DATE DUE

Technology, Investment and Growth

Technology, Investment and Growth

B. R. WILLIAMS

Vice-Chancellor, University of Sydney
New South Wales

CHAPMAN AND HALL LTD

11 NEW FETTER LANE · LONDON EC4

First published 1967
© Bruce R. Williams 1967
Printed in Great Britain by
C. Tinling & Co Ltd,
Liverpool, London and Prescot

DISTRIBUTED IN THE USA BY BARNES & NOBLE INC.

Contents

Contents

Foreword

Paul Samuelson once remarked that, if you listen to the speeches that scientists make when they take off their white laboratory coats, you might think that all the old rules of the game have to be scrapped, and all the principles of economics rewritten. Of some scientists this is fair comment. Yet, applied research and development is simply a form of investment, and in many cases a form of investment which cannot yield an economic return unless it is followed by a very much larger investment in plant and equipment and marketing. It also makes claims on scarce scientific and engineering manpower which can be used in a variety of employments. It is quite possible to hinder economic growth by employing too high a proportion of scientists and engineers in research and development. Finding the right deployment of scientific manpower is a part of the general economic problem.

In these general essays, selected from among those I have written on 'science and industry' in the past ten years, I have concentrated on the inter-relations of research and development and economic growth. In this way the logical consequences – 'the scarecrows of fools and the beacons of wise men' – of many of our present attitudes and policies can be set out fairly clearly.

The first essay is concerned with the 'technology gap'. A lot of nonsense is written about this gap. It cannot be measured directly, and if measured indirectly, by for example growth rates of output, the gap between the United States and West Europe is shrinking not growing. If measured instead by research and development expenditure the post-war gap has increased, but here the most obvious thing is the marked divergence between patterns of expenditure, due to the great increase in defence and space research and development in the United States. Neither the growth significance of this divergence in pattern nor the policy implications for West European countries are as yet clear – except I think negatively. Even if Western Europe learned to act as 'one nation' it could not match the United States in either wealth or supplies of scientists and engineers. A copy of the United States pattern of research and development would be an inferior copy. And particularly while the big United States advantage in the relevant resources remains it would reduce growth potential to impede significantly the Atlantic transfer of technology.

Parts of the argument in Chapter I are dealt with more fully in Chapters II–VII, and, for undeveloped countries, in Chapter XII. It helps to think of technological progress not simply in terms of *opportunities* created by research and development (wherever it may be performed), but also in terms of *capacities* to use these opportunities – a factor affected by the deployment of scientific manpower– and the *pressures* to innovate.

It is a recurring human weakness to present simple, single-factor explanations of very complex social problems. The main contemporary competitor to the simple research and development theory of growth is the investment rate theory. This is in fact a more general theory for, to the extent that technical progress has to enter industry through the investment process, investment in research and development is simply caught up in the more general investment explanation. I have criticized this approach in Chapters V and IX, and by implication in Chapters X and XI.

Chapter XIII on the automatic factory touches, rather sceptically, on some of the fears and forecasts concerning the 'age of automation'. The final chapter – a general plea for the wider use of cost-benefit analysis – includes some comments on the machinery of Government as it reflects Government policy concerning science and technology. There is some overlapping material in these essays and a certain amount of inconsistency, which I at first decided to edit out. That I did not was due, on the one hand, to a view gained as a university teacher that it often helps to present explanations in different contexts and, on the other hand, to indicate how quickly situations, or one's judgements of situations, can change. I note for example that I asked seriously in an essay written in 1956 (Chapter III) whether we should concentrate our research and development on a range of problems such as nuclear energy, aircraft, and electronics!

I wish to thank the Editors of *The New Scientist, The Times Review of Industry, The Yorkshire Bulletin of Economic and Social Studies, The Journal of Management Studies, The Journal of the Institution of Production Engineers, The Economic Journal,* and UNESCO for permission to republish Chapters IV, V, VI, X, XII, XIII, and XIV.

The University of Manchester   B.R.W.
May 1967

I

The Research Gap
and European Growth

What are the implications of the large research gap between West European countries and the United States, of West Europe's unfavourable balance of technological payments, of the very extensive United States foreign investment, of the migration of scientific manpower to the United States? Will the research gap give the United States an accumulating advantage in advanced technology and economic growth? Is the unfavourable technological balance of payments a sign that West European countries underinvest in research and development (RandD)? Does the rapidly growing United States direct investment in European industry mean that a growing proportion of 'European' firms will come to have only a sort of colonial status? In sum, are West European countries really in danger of becoming technological colonies of the United States?

I. THE RESEARCH GAP

Expenditure on RandD in the United States is very much higher than in any other country. The United States expenditure on RandD in 1962 was $15,610 million, 2·8% of the gross national product (GNP) at market price. In 1963 the expenditure was $17,350 million, 3·0% of GNP.[1] In the United Kingdom, expenditure on RandD was £650 million in 1961–2, and £770 million in 1964–5, approximately 2·3% of GNP at market price on both occasions. The United Kingdom expenditure in 1962 (converted in a necessarily approximate way from the 1961–2 basis in the light of the 1964–5 figures, and into dollars at the official exchange rate) was $1,850–1,900 million, less than one-eighth of the United States expenditure. Russian expenditure when converted into dollars at the official rates of exchange was only one-third, and the French and the West German only one-fourteenth, of the United States expenditure.[2]

However, the use of official rates of exchange gives a misleading impression of the research gap. The cost of conducting similar research varies between countries. To allow for this, Freeman and Young calculated a research rate of exchange for 1962, and although such a calculation is subject to fairly wide margins of error the use of it enables us to get a better idea of the real research gap. Whereas at the currency rate of exchange United Kingdom R and D was only 12% of that in the United States, at the research rate of exchange it was 22%. But even at the research rates of exchange, the total expenditure on R and D in the five western European countries was only 50% of that in the United States.

TABLE 1

Estimated Gross Expenditure on Research and Development, 1962
$ million

	RandD (currency rates of exchange)	RandD (research rates of exchange)	% of US RandD	% of GNP (market price)
USA	15,610	15,610	100	2·8
UK	1,875	3,375	22	2·3
France	1,108	1,660	11	1·5
West Germany	1,105	1,880	12	1·3
Netherlands	239	443	3	1·8
Belgium	113	225	2	1·0

R and D efforts in different countries do not only differ in amounts. They differ greatly in nature. In 1962 about 60% of R and D expenditure in the United States was for military and space, compared to about 50% in France, 40% in the United Kingdom, and 10% or less in West Germany, Netherlands, and Belgium. At the research exchange rate, United States military and space R and D was almost four times greater than that of the five West European countries together, seven to eight times greater than in the United Kingdom, ten times greater than in France, and fifty times greater than in West Germany. In purely civil R and D, the United States effort was less than one and a half times greater than West Europe's, though almost three and a half times greater than in the United Kingdom, four times greater than in West Germany, and eight times greater than in France.

It is easy to establish the general dimension of the R and D expenditure gap. The economic effects, and the policy implications, are much less straightforward.

The disparities in RandD expenditures were not reflected in growth rates of output per man employed. Allowing a time lag of five years between RandD expenditure and its effect on growth, we do not find evidence of a positive association between national research and growth. The average compound rate of growth in output per man employed 1955–64 in the United States was 1·9%, which was just 10% greater than its average RandD percentage in the years 1950–9. In the United Kingdom the growth percentage 1955–64 was 50% greater than the RandD percentage 1950–9. In West Germany and France the growth percentage was over seven times, and in Japan over fourteen times, the lagged RandD percentage.

Why then the worry about the RandD gap? The first reason may be West Europe's sense of insecurity following the vast military and space RandD of the United States (and Russia). In 1962 military and space RandD expenditure in the United States was seven to eight times greater than in the United Kingdom and ten times greater than in France. Here, as elsewhere, the results of the RandD process have to be applied to have effect; and in this field there are substantial economies of scale which no West European country is in a position to realize. The scale problem could be reduced to more manageable dimensions if West European countries combined for military and space RandD. However the total of West European space RandD was, at research rates of exchange, only 25% of that in the United States, and any attempt to match the American effort would create an acute shortage of scientific manpower in West Europe. In any case, the feeling that there is a specifically West European set of defence interests, which may conflict with the interests of the United States, has so far not been sufficiently strong to induce West European countries to act together in military and space RandD and production.

The second reason for worry about the research gap is due to the belief that economic growth depends on the level of research. Even when it is shown that this has not been so for individual countries (for reasons which are set out in Chapters III and VIII), the belief persists that it must somehow be so in the future. The mere absence of past statistical association between national expenditure on RandD and national growth does not of course provide proof that such an association will not emerge in the future. There are, however, good analytical grounds for believing that the past absence of correlation between national research and national growth was not pure chance. R and D is important for growth but the idea that a country's growth depends on its own R and D overlooks the great importance of the international movement of ideas, of machines which embody the results of R and D, and of capital transfers to make possible the use in various countries of technological and managerial inventions made elsewhere.*

If we look at the problem simply in terms of economic growth it is not difficult to see that the appropriate level of R and D will vary from country to country with the level of technology, the supply of scientific manpower, the industry mix, and the cost of importing new technological knowledge.

The lower the level of technology the greater will be the opportunity to grow by using technologies already established elsewhere. The level of output per man provides a very rough index of the level of technology achieved in different countries. Maddison's calculations are given in Table 2.

TABLE 2

	Real GNP (US relative prices)	OPM employed
	UK = 100	
USA	506	176
France	88	112
West Germany	112	110
UK	100	100
USSR	342	82
Japan	141	77

Source: Maddison, *Lloyds Bank Review,* January 1966.

In the United States, growth is more dependent on their own R and D than it is in West European countries, and still more so than in USSR and Japan.

The importance of the scientific manpower position is that scientists and engineers have alternative uses. They are needed both for making use of the existing stock of scientific and technological knowledge and for R and D. It follows that if two countries have similar levels of technology and industrial structure, it will pay the

* See Chapters VIII and IX.

country with the less favourable scientific manpower position to aim for a lower degree of self-sufficiency in the creation of opportunities for innovation. Because of different methods and standards of training, international comparisons of scientific manpower are subject to wide margins of error, but a rough indication of the position in 1962 is given in Table 3.[3]

TABLE 3

	QSE as % of US stock	QSE as % of employed population	% of QSE in R and D
USA	100	1·7	33
USSR	(120)	(1·8)	(20)
Japan	40	1·3	(15)
UK	20	1·0	25
West Germany	19	0·9	15
France	14	0·9	17

The United States and the USSR have the strongest position on scientific manpower, both absolutely and as a proportion of working population. The United States with its higher level of technology and greater dependence on its own R and D for growth has a higher proportion of its scientists and engineers employed in R and D. The United Kingdom with a lower level of technology than the United States and a less favourable scientific manpower position has a smaller percentage engaged in R and D.

Germany and France are very similar to the United Kingdom in levels of technology and in stock of scientists and engineers as a percentage of working population, but have significantly smaller percentages of scientific manpower engaged in R and D. Yet their growth rates have been higher, and there is no evidence that they have suffered from their greater use of scientists and engineers outside R and D. The position is complicated by military and space R and D which in 1962 was 60% of total R and D in France, 40% in the United Kingdom and 10% in West Germany. But given the very much greater cost of military and space R and D per scientist and engineer involved, the proportion of R and D scientists and engineers engaged on military and space R and D was very much smaller than the expenditure figures would suggest. In the United Kingdom it was approximately one-fifth, leaving 20% of scientific manpower engaged on civil R and D. In France and West Germany the percentage of scientific manpower engaged in civil R and D was in the region of 11–13%. The United Kingdom's high ratio of scientists and engineers engaged in R and D is not therefore simply a reflection of defence policy, except in so far as extensive Government support to civil aircraft R and D was motivated by a desire to maintain a form of production thought to have a substantial defence potential.

It is of course possible for two countries with the same R and D percentage to have very different R and D programmes. In 1962 the civil R and D percentage was very similar in the United States, the United Kingdom, and West Germany, and significantly below that in the Netherlands. It is also possible for two countries to spend on R and D the same percentage of net product in each industry and yet to have markedly different R and D percentages. This can happen because the industry mix varies from country to country. If for example we extracted from the United Kingdom figures aircraft R and D – which is very largely financed by the Government – the United Kingdom R and D percentage would be only 2%. The use of aggregated national R and D figures without reference to the growth objectives of the component parts and without reference to the industry mix has led to some deplorable generalizations (see Chapters IV and VIII).

Because scientific manpower has alternative uses, and a country's sources of innovation are not only generated by its own R and D, it is possible to impede growth by spending more on R and D. Finding the optimum distribution of scientific manpower is an important part of growth policy. When counting the cost of importing technology it is just as important to work out the growth implications of diverting a higher proportion of scientists and engineers to R and D work as to tot up the cost of licences and knowhow agreements. When this is done there is certainly no general reason to believe that the United Kingdom's growth prospects would be improved by stepping up its R and D expenditure and increasing the proportion of scientists and engineers engaged in R and D. There are some very effective procedures for spreading new technologies about the world. This is one of the main reasons why relatively small or poor countries which cannot possibly match the R and D expenditure of larger or richer countries are able to achieve high growth rates.

However some of the worry about the research gap is based on a desire to reduce the importance of this international mechanism for transmitting economic growth opportunities, on grounds either that the growth effects of this mechanism are greater in the short run than in the long run, or that growth should be restricted in the interests of nationalism. This provides the context for examination of, first, the technological balance of payments, and, second, foreign direct investment.

2. THE TECHNOLOGICAL BALANCE OF PAYMENTS

Statistics on payments for and receipts from the sale of knowhow and patent rights are used in two ways – to calculate the burden of payments which could (or might) be reduced by greater R and D expenditure, and to give some indication of comparative national levels of technological knowledge in different fields. In both cases the statistics need to be handled with some care: some international companies make a specific charge to overseas branches for knowhow and patent rights and some do not, and the problem of a specific charge for licensing or the use of knowhow does not arise when the innovating companies embody the innovation in their own output. This last point could be of great significance. For some countries may, because of their cost position at home or other difficulties in exporting goods, have a greater interest than other countries in seeking royalty and knowhow fees abroad. This appears to be the position in the United States, and to the extent that this is so statistics of the 'technological balance of payments' will not reflect the relative states of technological eminence. Indeed, in general, changes in the statistics over time will be rather more significant than the figures in any one year. Unfortunately, reliable time series do not exist.

In the United Kingdom the results of the first annual enquiry were published in *The Board of Trade Journal* of 29th July, 1966. Allowing for non-response, it was estimated that receipts from technological 'royalties, licences, patents, manufacturing rights, or any similar arrangements' amounted to £44·0 million and payments to £41·1 million. If this is the correct figure, the United Kingdom has a slight surplus of payments over receipts.

TABLE 4

United Kingdom Overseas Royalties Transactions, 1964
£ million

	Receipts	Expenditure
Technological royalties	44·0	41·1
Royalties on books, recordings, etc.	13·9	8·8
Mineral royalties	1·0	0·4
	58·9	50·3

Table 5 gives a regional analysis of these transactions. In this case the Board of Trade statisticians have made no allowance for non-response, and the table is based directly on the figures returned by the firms which responded to the enquiry.

TABLE 5

Area Analysis of United Kingdom Technological Royalty Transactions
£ million

		Receipts		Expenditure	
USA		6·0		24·4	
EEC		8·3		5·6	
	of which France		2·2		3·6
	West Germany		3·7		1·0
EFTA		1·8		3·4	
	of which Switzerland		0·3		2·3
Other countries		16·4		0·6	
		32·5		34·0	

Here there was a slight surplus of payments over receipts. Payments to the United States were four times greater than receipts, which fits the thesis that countries with a high rate of expenditure on R and D will have a 'favourable technological balance of payments', and vice versa. The fact that France and Switzerland had 'favourable balances' with the United Kingdom does not, however, fit in with the thesis, though it would be reasonable to argue here that we should look at the overall position for a country and not simply to its balance with separate countries.

For West Germany there is information from 1950 published in the *Bundesbank Bulletin*.

TABLE 6

West German Receipts from and Payments to Foreign Countries
for Inventions, Processes, Copyrights, etc.
DM millions

	Receipts	Expenditure	Balance
1950	10	22	− 12
1955	76	222	− 146
1960	155	520	− 355
1961	169	629	− 450
1962	186	631	− 445
1963	216 (199)	637 (541)	− 421

For 1963 it was possible to exclude copyrights and the figures net of copyright are given in brackets. The area analysis of payments and receipts is given in Table 7.

TABLE 7

West German Receipts from and Payments to Foreign Countries on Patents, etc. (excluding copyrights), 1963
DM millions

	Receipts		Expenditure	
USA	41·7		207·2	
Asia	42·9		0·8	
of which Japan		36·0		0·7
Europe	93·2		323·4	
of which France		16·1		17·2
Italy		23·4		4·7
Netherlands		5·4		45·4
Switzerland		4·6		155·5
UK		15·5		71·9
Other countries	13·7		8·3	
All countries	198·9		541·4	

Expenditure on technological licences and knowhow was 2·7 times greater than receipts in 1963. With the United States, expenditure was five times greater than receipts (perhaps more, in view of the use by some United States companies at that time of the Swiss 'tax haven'). Of particular interest is the fall in the surplus of expenditure over receipts since 1961. German patent and licensing rights were largely confiscated during the war, and inevitably receipts built up slowly after the war. But since 1958 receipts have grown at a faster rate (85%) than expenditure (75%).

In the period 1960–2, French payments grew significantly relative to receipts. In 1962, payments were about F 535 million and receipts F 200 million, giving as in West Germany (1963) an overall ratio of payments to receipts of 2·7. Payments to the United States were $53 million and receipts $11 million – a ratio of payments to receipts of 4·8, compared to the West German ratio of 5·2 (in 1963) and the United Kingdom ratio of 4·1 (in 1964).

The figures for the United States are of a different order. In 1961 receipts were $577 million and payments $63 million; in 1962 $760 million and $80 million. In both years, payments were just over 10% of receipts (though a higher percentage in transactions with the United Kingdom, France, and West Germany).

B

The overall ratios of payments to receipts – approximately 0·1 for the United States in 1962, 1·0 for the United Kingdom in 1964, and 2·7 for West Germany in 1963 and France 1962 – are consistent with the thesis that the technological balance of payments roughly reflects the level of expenditure on R and D. But it should not be deduced from this that it would pay the United Kingdom to spend more on R and D to create a more 'favourable' balance of technological payments, or pay West Germany and France to spend a great deal more on R and D to eliminate their 'unfavourable' technological balance of payments. The United States position is the result both of the overall level of R and D and of its better relative supply of scientific manpower (Table 3). Furthermore in both France and Germany payments for licences and knowhow in 1962 were only 10%, and receipts less than 4% and 5% respectively of expenditure on R and D. In the United Kingdom receipts and payments in 1964 were just under 5% of R and D. Given that payments for patent rights and knowhow are generally only made when there is a proven impact on technology, it is clear that the case for considerably greater R and D expenditure simply on grounds of the technological balance of payments is very weak.

It is unfortunate that the concept of the technological balance of payments has been popularized. For it implies that any unfavourable balance – a surplus of payments over receipts – is a sign of maladjustment that should be corrected. This is not so. The technological balance of payments is only one (very incomplete) indication of the international movement of technology. The extent to which any country can do effective R and D across the board is largely a function of the size of its scientific manpower. The extent to which it will pay any country to 'import technology' depends on its existing level of technology, the size of its scientific manpower, and the extent of its growth objectives. The balance between self reliance and dependence will vary from industry to industry with such things as the ratio of R and D cost to unit production cost, the ratio of scientists to engineers (which affects a country's relative efficiency as between fields which depend more on science than on engineering and vice versa), and relative degrees of patent protection.

3. FOREIGN INVESTMENT

The transmission of new or improved technologies via licence and knowhow agreements is not entirely separate from the transmission via foreign direct investment. More than one-half of the United States receipts from the sale of licences and knowhow to Europe comes from charges to 'direct investment companies'.[4]

United States direct investments abroad were valued at $11,788,000,000 in 1950. By the end of 1965, direct investment had risen to $49,217,000,000.[5] The main geographical distribution of these direct investments is given in Table 8. The biggest growth was in Europe. The United Kingdom's share rose from 7% to 10%, and Europe's as a whole from 15% of the total in 1950 to 27% in 1964.

TABLE 8

United States Direct Investments Abroad
$ million

	1950	1957	1961	1962	1963	1965
Canada	3,579	8,769	11,602	12,133	13,044	15,172
Latin America	4,445	7,434	8,236	8,424	8,662	9,371
Common Market	637	1,680	3,104	3,722	4,470	6,254
UK	847	1,974	3,554	3,824	4,172	5,119
Africa	287	664	1,064	1,271	1,426	1,904
Middle East	692	1,138	1,240	1,200	1,277	1,590
Far East	309	881	1,237	1,300	1,515	2,021
Oceania	256	698	1,108	1,271	1,460	1,811

Source: *Survey of Current Business*, August 1964 and September 1966.

The Bundesbank recently estimated that the American share in the nominal capital of West German public companies was about 5%.[6] When allowance is made for companies not quoted on the Stock Exchange the share comes below 5%. No similar estimate has been made for France or the United Kingdom. However, at the end of 1964 the value of United States direct investment in the United Kingdom was $4,550 million compared to $2,077 million in West Germany and $1,437 million in France. The United States share in the nominal capital of all United Kingdom companies is probably in the region of 7–10%, though the share is higher in chemicals, machinery and vehicles where United States direct investment is concentrated.

A better indication of the importance of United States ownership is given by the sales of United States subsidiaries. The sales of United States manufacturing subsidiaries in the United Kingdom rose from 5–6% of manufacturing sales in 1957 to 9–10% in 1964. However, as the sales of United Kingdom manufacturing subsidiaries include sales of goods imported for re-sale without further manufacture – a proportion of which would have been imported anyway – the true percentage is nearer 9% than 10%.

TABLE 9

Sales of United States Manufacturing Subsidiaries
$ million

	1957	*1959*	*1961*	*1963*	*1965*	% *increase 1957–65*
Europe of which	6,313	7,690	10,780	14,045	18,761	197
UK	3,303	4,050	5,070	5,918	7,510	127
Germany	1,116	1,572	2,265	3,130	4,356	290
France	763	789	1,255	2,003	2,665	244

Source: *Survey of Current Business*, November 1965 and 1966.

The statistics on plant and equipment expenditure of United States subsidiaries give a further indication of the importance of United States firms and of their potential rate of growth.

In the main areas of expenditure – petroleum and manufacturing – the totals for the United Kingdom, France, Germany, Italy, and Netherlands are given in Table 10.

TABLE 10

Plant and Equipment Expenditures of United States Direct Foreign Investments in Petroleum and Manufacturing
$ million

	1963	*1964*	*1965*	*1966**
UK	539	627	830	978
France	216	244	318	413
West Germany	445	400	596	776
Italy	192	229	186	243
Netherlands	91	108	101	182

Source: *Survey of Current Business*, September 1965 and 1966.
* Based on company projections.

In 1963 and 1964 the proportion of United States controlled plant and equipment expenditure was just over 10% in the United Kingdom, under 5% in France, Germany, and Italy and over 5% in Netherlands. But the proportions are rising in the United Kingdom, France, West Germany, and Netherlands.

The scale of United States investment abroad has had a profound effect on world trade. Sales by United States direct-investment enterprises abroad are now approximately four times greater than the value of United States exports. In 1950, production abroad was about $13,000 million larger than exports; by 1964 the gap had grown to $64,000 million.[7]

The extent of this overseas investment has caused concern to the United States administration. Since 1963 the United States Government has operated a *Voluntary Program* of foreign investment and credit restraints in the expectation that this will strengthen the dollar – both directly, and indirectly through a check to the substitution of production abroad for commodity exports.

The belief that United States production abroad impedes United States exports was one very important reason for the post-war welcome given to United States investment in Europe. Other reasons were the shortage of native investible funds and the desire to increase investment, the capacity of United States firms to introduce improved and new technologies, and the desire to improve the geographical distribution of industry.

The encouragement to United States investment was certainly successful. Direct United States investment in the United Kingdom has grown rapidly from $847 million in 1950 to $5,119 million in 1965. The production of United States subsidiaries in the United Kingdom now amounts to almost three-quarters of the level of imports. It would have been impossible to import from the United States on this sort of scale. The importance of plant and equipment expenditure of United States subsidiaries was given in Table 10. A substantial part of this expenditure was financed from the inflow of capital and undistributed profits of the subsidiaries. Table 11 gives information for Europe on direct investment capital flows from the United States and on undistributed subsidiary earnings. Assuming that depreciation funds provided for maintenance of plant, 55% of funds for expansion of manufacturing were provided from retained profits and capital inflows in 1962, and 48% in 1963 and 1964. The reliance on non-United States finance was rather lower in the United Kingdom.

TABLE 11

Sources of Funds of United States Direct Foreign Investments in Europe
$ million

Retained profit			Funds from US			Funds from Europe			Depreciation		
1962	*1963*	*1964*	*1962*	*1963*	*1964*	*1962*	*1963*	*1964*	*1962*	*1963*	*1964*
Total											
221	401	368	557	577	765	608	1,111	1,167	696	810	990
Manufacturing											
215	401	426	299	239	383	410	681	862	475	571	735
Petroleum											
6	3	-47	255	331	380	198	431	305	220	237	250

Source: *Survey of Current Business*, November 1965.

There is ample evidence that the United States subsidiaries have introduced new and improved technologies[8] and increased the growth rate, and that United States investment has been used to improve the distribution of industry. Despite all this, there have been growing doubts in recent years about the wisdom of continuing to encourage 'inward investment', or, at least, about the wisdom of an unselective encouragement of inward investment.

There are many reasons for this shift of opinion. Nationalism has played an important part though in a rather complex way. For while it is argued that the sheer size of United States investment has made many important sectors of the economy 'dependent on the decisions of foreigners', it is also argued (sometimes by the same people) that if we joined the Common Market and if the Common Market developed a common defence R and D and procurement policy, and a common company law so that genuine European companies could be formed, then both the effective United States dominance in R and D, and the increase in United States investment in Europe, would be greatly diminished. Fear that United States firms will suppress competition from native firms in advanced-technology industries, and use the 'brain drain' to weaken our inventive capacity, has also helped to shift opinion. The United States firms have been cast in the role of the foxes (if not the little foxes) that spoil our vines. And, finally, apprehension about the balance of payments has played a part. The inflow of dollars helps the balance of payments at the time, but it is followed by the payment of interest, dividends, royalties, and management fees. And if United States subsidiaries have a high import content and a limited export franchise to suit the interests of the parent company, then the short term benefit to the balance of payments could be at the expense of long term interests.

4. NATIONAL INDEPENDENCE

It is extraordinarily difficult to give a precise meaning to the concept of 'undue dependence on foreigners', Any country so dependent on foreign trade as the United Kingdom, and which gives such emphasis in economic policy to full employment and high rates of economic growth, is necessarily dependent on foreigners in marked degree. The real problem is to find and move towards the forms of dependence which are most likely to enable us to reach our objectives. In these terms there is not much point in arguing in general that we have become unduly dependent on foreigners when we have been enabled by the import of foreign capital, technology, and managerial skill to substitute home production for imports, improve our export potential, and make possible a higher growth rate than would otherwise have been possible. There is point, however, in arguing against the import of foreign capital and technology in particular fields if there is good reason to believe that by feasible changes in industrial structure, management efficiency, the supply of scientists and technologists and the programming of R and D, we could improve our growth potential at smaller cost. The continuance of recent rates of increase in the proportion of United States ownership would give a clear indication that we were failing to make necessary reforms in industrial structure and managerial efficiency,[9] and failing to increase the supply of scientists and engineers at an economically advantageous rate.

The share of United States ownership of physical assets in the United Kingdom appears to be less than $2\frac{1}{2}\%$,[10] though it is 6–8% of business assets. The United States share of plant and equipment expenditure is over 10%. The fear that this interest is already high enough to create an unstable situation, in that in time of depression the United States parent firms would switch production to home plants and so impoverish the United Kingdom, is probably misplaced. The very scale of United States productive capacity abroad relative to capacity at home has created a greater identity of interest between the parent firms and the activity of their foreign subsidiaries than existing during the 1930's.

The rate of growth in United States direct investments in Europe must bear some relationship to the rate of profit. The United States Department of Commerce has estimated that the returns to United States firms from direct investments in Europe were higher than those in United States domestic manufacturing until 1963.[11]

Chart 1

Return on United States Manufacturing Investments

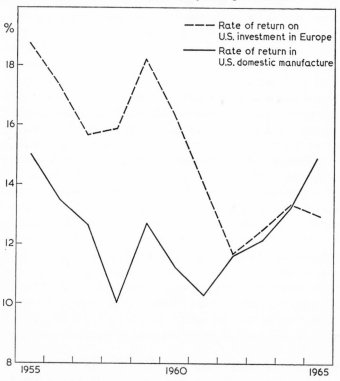

Source: *Survey of Current Business*, September 1966.

The coming together of these two profit rates does not of itself create a presumption that the inflow of United States capital to Europe will fall off. For there is little direct evidence that a differential profit rate is sufficient to induce a company to make direct investments abroad, and still less to suggest that a company with substantial direct investments abroad would discontinue the investment required for the maintenance of its market position simply because the differential disappeared.[12] What would check the inflow would be evidence that the return to further investment would be inadequate, and what would check growth in the proportion of United States ownership would be a rise in the ability of European industries to exploit the opportunities for profitable expansion as well as the United States firms. But, what, it may be asked, if United States firms are in a position to adopt strategies which ensure their dominance in the advanced-technology industries such as aircraft, electronic components and equipment, computers and tele-communications?

5. COMPETITIVE STRATEGIES

These happen to be areas in which United States commodity exports dwarf United States production abroad. But United States firms might still decide to invest enough abroad, particularly in the form of take-overs, to prevent the emergence of strong foreign competition. In Tektronix's Annual Report for 1964 such a strategy is outlined:

> Manufacturing within the major European trading areas lets us provide customers there with our instruments at lower prices (by avoiding restrictive trade barriers). It does another important thing: it acts to guard our United States markets against foreign manufacturers, who protected by trade barriers from vigorous competition in their own market or trade areas, could grow strong enough there to make inroads here also.[13]

In the explanation of United States investment overseas, great emphasis is sometimes given to the difficulties which large firms have in expanding their share of the home market against the competition of the other few firms in the industry. From this, it is said, follow decisions to seek opportunities abroad, and to reduce competition and increase profits by acquiring control over foreign enterprises.

The desire to extend sales abroad following difficulty in expanding market shares at home does not explain why such firms decide to *produce* abroad. Nor is the desire to reduce competition by taking over foreign firms a sufficient explanation of direct investment. Take-overs may simply provide the cheapest and quickest way to get started once a decision has been taken to produce abroad. Important factors encouraging direct investment abroad have been tariffs, import controls, lower production costs, high transport costs, local control of distribution outlets, and the advantages in being close to markets where good marketing requires attention to servicing the product. These factors also have an importance in industries which are not oligopolistic, and indeed in recent years there has been a rapid increase in the number of medium-sized United States firms which have made direct investments in Europe.

To get this problem into the right perspective it is important to keep in mind that investing abroad and taking over foreign firms is not an activity restricted to the Americans. Foreign direct investments in the United States itself are very extensive. The position in three post-war years is set out in Table 12. Foreign direct investments in the United States, and United Kingdom direct investments in the United States, more than doubled between 1950 and 1964.

TABLE 12

Foreign Direct Investments in the United States
$ million

	1950	*1960*	*1965*
Total	3,391	6,910	8,812
Europe	2,227	5,491	6,105
UK	1,168	2,248	2,865
Canada	1,029	1,934	2,367
Netherlands	334	947	1,304
Switzerland	348	773	938
Other Europe	477	739	998

Source: *Survey of Current Business*, September 1965 and 1966.

European direct investment in the United States at the end of 1965 was 55% of United States direct investment in Europe. United Kingdom direct investments in the United States at $2,865 million (or rather more if allowance is made for the fact that the Unilever direct investments in the United States are formally owned by the Netherlands section of the firm) were 56% of United States direct investments in the United Kingdom, although the physical assets of the United Kingdom are less than 20% of the United States figure.

The reasons given by United Kingdom firms for this direct investment – freight costs, servicing, tariff barriers, production costs, insight into United States technical developments, and the enforced abandonment of licensing agreements with United States firms – are not greatly dissimilar from those given by United States firms setting up in Europe.[14]

United Kingdom firms also have substantial direct investments in France and West Germany. The Bundesbank estimated the book value of United Kingdom direct investments in West Germany as $275 million in 1964. United Kingdom and Netherlands direct investments together were 80% of United States direct investments in Germany and 50% in France.

There is then nothing unique about the fact that United States firms invest overseas. And in the main this United States direct investment in Europe has increased competition. In both the United Kingdom and West Germany the bulk of United States direct investment has been in industries where there had been relatively little competition in the past. And judging from the post-war history of vehicles, chemicals, and oil refining, European firms can adapt themselves in a variety of ways to meet this stronger competition.

This does not mean that Governments can sit back in the safe knowledge that they can rely on a 'countervailing power' process. Where there is a great disproportion between the financial resources of the firms involved effective competition might lead the dominant firm – General Motors let us suppose – to think in terms of take-overs to restrict competition. If that did happen, Government action against restraint of trade would be called for. Given the United States laws on restraint of trade, the presence of more than one United States firm (e.g. Chrysler, Ford, and General Motors in vehicles) provides a safeguard against such anti-competition moves (though not against the growth of United States firms relative to national firms).

Where the United States investment is not into an established field, but into a new field where they have a dominant position (e.g. computers and certain electronic capital goods) the 'counter-vailing power' process in the private sphere may be far too weak. Token production abroad, and large discounts to strategically important buyers, may be deliberately designed to protect a manufacturing dominance (based on an original technological lead) which could otherwise be lost quite quickly.[15]

Evidence of a competitive policy by United States firms designed to prevent the emergence of competitive firms would provide a case for Government action against it and measures to encourage national firms – so long as there was also evidence that these firms, perhaps after amalgamations which brought potential sales into line with the necessary level of development costs, could soon meet genuine competition. Otherwise such Government action would only lead to a misuse of part of our scarce scientific and engineering manpower.

6. POLARIZATION OF RESEARCH AND DEVELOPMENT?

Another possible form of unfair competition would arise from United States take-overs if they were associated with the withdrawal of Rand D manpower and facilities from Europe to the United States. That there are some strong polarizing tendencies in the conduct of Rand D is indicated by the flow of European and Asiatic Rand D scientists and engineers to the United States, by the concentration of Russian Rand D near Moscow and Leningrad, and of French Rand D near Paris.

Table 13 gives information on the migration to the United States of those calling themselves scientists and engineers. For the United Kingdom the number of *qualified* engineers in the quoted 507 was less than 200. Comparable corrections may need to be made for the other countries. The second half of the table, which is often quoted in discussions of the brain drain, is seriously misleading. For the United Kingdom, 'qualified' emigrants as a percentage of new supply, given in Cmnd. 3007, was about $2\frac{1}{2}\%$ for engineers and overall, not $17\cdot4\%$ and $7\cdot4\%$. But, although the dimension of the problems has been grossly inflated, there is a problem – there has recently been some increase in the brain drain to the United States and there is some evidence that the emigrants included a high proportion of the most able scientists and engineers.[16]

TABLE 13
Migration of Scientists and Engineers to the United States

	Immigrants into the US annual average 1956–61			Emigrants as percentage of output: science and engineering graduates 1959		
	Scientists	*Engineers*	*Total*	*Scientists*	*Engineers*	*Total*
All countries	1,114	3,755	4,868			
All Europe	549	1,684	2,233			
France	26	56	82	0·5	1·2	0·9
Germany	124	301	425	6·0	9·8	8·2
Netherlands	34	102	136	7·9	21·8	15·1
UK	155	507	661	2·6	17·2	7·4
				2·5	8·7	5·4

Source: Freeman and Young, *The Research and Development Effort* (*OECD*, 1965). For corrections, see the text above.

Fears that United States direct investment in Europe will intensify the attraction of scientists and engineers to the United States were increased by the publication of the Stanford Research Institute's *Long Range Planning Report, 198*. It reported of a representative sample of 200 United States firms, that although one-half of them undertook R and D in Europe, most spent 4% or less of their own R and D budget there. The report indicated that many United States firms regard their European research primarily as a means for the effective monitoring of European R and D and of gaining entry to the European scientific community. (The same comment could be made of much United Kingdom-company R and D in the United States.)

There is no evidence, however, that there has been a net withdrawal of R and D facilities to the United States. Where United States firms have taken over United Kingdom firms they have frequently increased R and D expenditure in the United Kingdom. There are indeed some indications that United States firms may in the future undertake a considerably higher proportion of their research in Europe, which move may increase the shortage of scientists and engineers available to genuine European firms more than the present loss of scientists and engineers by emigration (see Table 14).

TABLE 14

Research and Development as Percentage of Net Output in United States Subsidiaries and All United Kingdom Firms, 1961

	US subsidiaries	All UK firms
Chemicals	4·8	4·5
Office machinery	16·3	2·3
Instruments	3·4	6·0
Vehicles	6·2	1·4
Machine tools	6·4	2·3
Other non-electrical engineering	8·6	2·3
Electrical engineering	4·8	5·6
Food, drink and tobacco	2·5	0·3
Other manufacturing	4·2	0·6

Source: J. H. Dunning, 'United States Subsidiaries in Britain and their United Kingdom Competitors' to be published in *Business Ratios*, Autumn 1966.

The emigration of United Kingdom scientists and engineers to the United States is not a new problem. Given the size of their R and D resources, the levels of income, the similarities of language and culture, there is likely to be a net emigration in the foreseeable future. Given our levels of technology and scientific manpower the solution to the problem is not just to pour more money into United Kingdom RandD. What appears to be needed is more selectivity in RandD, and more efficiency in applying science and technology to industry, involving as it does a different attitude to the role of scientific manpower in design and development, production and marketing. Because we have spread our RandD effort too widely and because size groupings are often inappropriate, we have very many RandD departments which are too small to be effective in generating profits. Because of this ineffectiveness, salaries and facilities are kept in a relatively poor state. The slower we are to increase the efficient use of scientific manpower and to generate a higher rate of growth, the slower will we be in raising the status and income of scientists and engineers and stopping their movement to the United States.

One factor of importance in the emigration of scientists and engineers is that some interesting fields of RandD have become too expensive in money and manpower for a country the size of the United Kingdom. The same is true of other West European countries. This has led to the suggestion that such RandD should be organized on a European basis. Indeed it has been argued frequently these days that unless Europe combines in this way it will not be able to stay in the field of advanced technology.

Such co-operation is already practised by countries which recognize the need for partnership. There is already a certain amount of co-operation in space and nuclear research, and in aircraft France and the United Kingdom have taken co-operation beyond research to the actual production stage. However the problems of effective European co-operation in the fields of advanced technology are formidable. It is relatively easy to co-operate in basic research. But if Europe is to get value for money in aerospace and electronics it will be necessary to go far beyond co-operation in research to co-operation in development, production and purchasing. Because in aerospace and many fields of electronics RandD costs are large relative to production costs, a large market for the product is required for economical production, and because of this co-operation in purchasing, e.g. defence equipment, aircraft and computers, may be an essential part of the whole operation. Such co-operation will not be at all easy to achieve. Nor for that matter will it be easy to achieve effective co-operation in development and production. Efficiency requires a close association between development and production – there is plenty of evidence from the United Kingdom experience of the cost of segregating development from production – and the critical problem in international collaboration is to ensure that the various national teams have parts of the project which are largely independent and yet have interconnections which do not involve complex scientific or engineering problems. Economically effective co-operation will probably require the growth of genuinely European companies (whether State or private) to which at the moment there are many barriers, although as we know from the history of Unilever and Shell, not impassable barriers.

If West European Governments decide to co-operate in areas of technology where it is uneconomic for single countries but economic for several countries acting together, then a properly staffed 'technological community' could play an important part. Such a community could help to define the areas of profitable collaboration. It could make clear the dangers of a political carve-up of the work, demonstrate the need to base division of labour on sound engineering and financial principles, and provide expert advice on the placing of research, development, and production contracts. It could give advice on any changes in the structure of industry required to make best use of modern technology, and it could help to facilitate agreements on such important matters as standards and patent procedures.

7. BALANCE OF PAYMENTS

The inflow of United States capital to finance direct investment strengthens the demand for sterling at the time of the inflow. Any subsequent import-saving or export-creating production also strengthens sterling. On the other hand, the payments of dividends, management fees, and royalties to the United States and any increase of imports due simply to the existence of the United States parent company – an effect likely to be strongest where the direct investments are in distribution facilities – have offsetting effects.

It is not possible to put numbers against some of these effects. This is partly because of inadequate statistical information. But the main reason is that we cannot know what the United Kingdom economy would now be like if the United States investment had not taken place. If there had been strong impediments to foreign direct investment, United States export policy might have been more aggressive in third markets, there might have been more licence and knowhow agreements with United Kingdom firms, the shift of resources into industries with a greater export potential than our traditional export industries might not have gone so far. The most that can be done is to use the numbers that do exist to test the plausibility of the balance-of-payments arguments for and against United States investment. A starting point is the information on the proportion of United States exports which go to affiliated companies.

TABLE 15

United States Exports to Europe
$ million

	1962	1963	1964
1. US exports to Europe	7,106	7,598	[8,200]
2. Exports to US affiliates in Europe	1,541	1,507	1,813
3. of which: petroleum	127	119	131
4. manufacturing	721	811	1,029
5. trade	610	472	493
6. other industries	83	105	160
7. Line 2 as % of line 1	22%	20%	[22%]

Source: *Survey of Current Business*, December 1965.

By no means all these exports are tied to the activities of the United States subsidiaries in the sense that they would cease if the United States subsidiaries were sold to nationals. The object of the 'trade' subsidiaries is to sell more goods, or to sell them on better terms to the parent company, than would otherwise be possible. Manufacturing subsidiaries are also used to distribute some parent company goods without further manufacture. Such United States exports amounted to a high percentage of the total exports to affiliated companies – $1,124 million in 1962, $1,084 million in 1963, and $1,175 million in 1964. The United States firms would lose only a portion of these exports if the subsidiaries were sold and other arrangements were made for distribution.

But if any part of these exports is dependent on direct overseas investment, the effect is to raise the import content of United States firms in Europe. It is not possible to calculate this effect. But it is known that goods imported from parent companies by European subsidiaries of United States companies for 'resale without further manufacture' were only $2\frac{1}{2}\%$ of their sales. Total imports by United

States subsidiaries in Europe from parent companies were in the region of 6% of sales and 25% of exports. These figures are given in Table 16.

TABLE 16

Sales of United States Manufacturing Subsidiaries in Europe
$ million

	1962	1963	1964
1. Sales of US manufacturing affiliates in Europe	12,020	14,015	16,500
2. Imports from US	721	811	1,029
3. Line 2 as % of line 1	6%	5·8%	6·2%
4. Exports of US affiliates in Europe	2,646	3,233	3,789
5. Line 4 as % of line 1	22%	23%	21%

Source: *Survey of Current Business*, November 1965.

For the United Kingdom there is published information on the sales of United States subsidiaries but not on imports from the United States. But if the percentages given in Line 3 of Table 16 apply also to the United Kingdom, the position would be as shown in Table 17.

TABLE 17

Sales of United States Manufacturing Subsidiaries in United Kingdom
$ million

	1962	1963	1964
Sales of US manufacturing subsidiaries	5,265	5,960	6,910
Imports from the US	(316)	(346)	(426)
Exports*	(1,316)	(1,490)	(1,727)

* Estimated by assuming that percentage of sales is the same as for 1965.

The sales of United States manufacturing subsidiaries include the 're-sale without further manufacture' of goods imported from the United States. Some of these goods were doubtless exported to other European countries, but as these goods only amounted (at United States export values) to $2\frac{1}{2}$% of the value of sales, adjustment

c

of the statistics to the basis of United Kingdom (or European) production exported would not be significant.

The export performance of the European manufacturing subsidiaries of United States companies is quite impressive. In 1965 the percentage of turnover exported was 27 in West Germany, 25 in the United Kingdom, 17 in France and 14 in Italy. These exports were a significant part of manufactured exports in each country – almost 17% in the United Kingdom, 7% in West Germany, 6% in France and 3% in Italy.[18]

A very small proportion of these exports goes to the United States. Of the exports given in Line 4 in Table 16 only $135 million went to the United States in 1962, $121 million in 1963, and $208 million in 1964. Indeed only Canadian affiliates of United States companies made large exports to the United States ($1,227 million out of a total of $1,636 million in 1964) and these consisted primarily of products of natural resource industries. There is nothing very surprising in these figures, though they do indicate that the extent to which 'United States companies have switched part of their United States production to the United Kingdom (and other European countries) in order, not only to further their overseas markets, but to increase their domestic competitive position by importing (from their own subsidiaries) materials, parts or finished products more cheaply than they could have been produced in the United States'[17] has been quite small.

It is not possible to calculate the import content of United States production in Europe from the information given in Table 16. From sales and imports we need to deduct some part of imported goods for re-sale without further manufacture. To this must be added the imports from other sources. Judging from Dunning's 1957 study, the ratio of imported bought-out raw materials and semi-manufactured goods would have been less than 6·5% of sales revenue in 1964 after some rough calculations on the basis of the import content in the relevant United Kingdom industries, I decided to calculate imports as 10% of sales.

Information on the payment of all interest, dividends, royalties, and management fees to North America is given in the *United Kingdom Balance of Payments 1966*. Using this information in conjunction with Department of Commerce information on the payment of royalty and management fees by United States manufacturing subsidiaries in Europe, guesstimates have been made for United Kingdom manufacturing subsidiaries. These are given in Table 18 together with estimates for exports.

TABLE 18

Transactions of United States Manufacturing Subsidiaries in United Kingdom
£ million

	1962	1963	1964
Exports	(460)	(530)	(620)
Imports	(180)	(210)	(250)
Royalties and management fees	(40)	(60)	(90)
Remitted profits	(40)	(40)	(70)

Assuming these guesstimates are reasonably near the mark, the United States manufacturing subsidiaries produced an average annual export surplus of £200 million. To get the total effect on the flow of payments we must add the annual capital imports of the United States manufacturing subsidiaries of over £50 million. If all the production had been financed by United States capital, and it was production that would not otherwise have taken place, we could then say that the direct improvement in the flow of payments due to United States investment is in the region of £250 million a year. In fact some of the capital inflow has been used to take over existing United Kingdom firms (in which case the favourable effect is limited to the capital inflow and any increase in net exports), and some of the United States production has been financed by loans raised in the United Kingdom (in which case there is no capital inflow but an outflow of post-interest profits). Allowing for these factors, the direct favourable impact on the balance of payments might have been as low as £200 million in recent years. But this is still a high figure.

For reasons already given, the calculation of indirect effects – the favourable effects of producing here what would otherwise have been imported, and the stimulus to more efficient performance by United Kingdom manufacturers, and the unfavourable effects of limited export franchises and checks to the rapid expansion of United Kingdom firms in or into certain growth fields – would degenerate still further from guesstimates to guesses.

8. CONCLUSIONS

(*a*) That the United States R and D effort is very much larger than in other countries – almost five times greater than in the United Kingdom, and more than twice the combined effort in Britain, France, and West Germany – does not mean that the growth rate in GNP in the United States will dwarf that in other countries. The existence of this large research gap does not of itself create a case for greater expenditure on R and D. Indeed, because scientific manpower has alternative uses, and a country's opportunities for innovation are not generated only from its own R and D, it is possible to impede growth by spending more on R and D. There is not good reason to believe that the United Kingdom's growth prospects would be improved by increasing the proportion of scientific manpower engaged in R and D. But, because the United Kingdom's scientific manpower, at about one-fifth of the United States', is far too small for an effective effort in all fields of R and D, there is good reason to believe that the United Kingdom's growth prospects would be improved by a further concentration of effort. The effort should be concentrated rather more in those fields of technology where the scientific and market growth potential is good, where, in view of Britain's relatively better supply of scientists than of engineers, the scientific content of final production is high, and where the ratio of development cost to competitive unit production cost is appropriate to the United Kingdom's potential market.

(*b*) If West European countries co-operated fully, the gap between the United States and European R and D efforts would be much smaller. In 1962 the United States civil R and D effort was only 50% greater than the West European, though about four times greater in military and space R and D. Certainly with full co-operation the dominance of the United States in aircraft and electronic capital goods (including computers) could be reduced. But it is important to emphasize what 'full co-operation' entails. It is not enough to set up institutions like, e.g. Euratom, as a simple addition to independent national atomic energy authorities. Nor is it enough to get Governments to agree projects like Concord and very big computers, and then divide up the work among independent national firms. For effective developments in such fields the growth of West European firms (whether State or private) and the co-ordination of State purchasing will be needed. The political problems here are obviously very formidable.

(*c*) One very important reason why there is not a high correlation between national levels of expenditure on R and D and growth rates is that there are effective mechanisms for spreading new technology about the world through licence and knowhow agreements, the export of equipment embodying the new technology, and direct investment in foreign countries. The extent to which it pays a country to rely on 'importing new technology' rather than trying to create it all at home, depends on its existing level of technology, the size of its scientific manpower and the extent of its specialization in production. In general it is foolish for a country with relatively low levels of technology and scientific manpower to worry about an 'unfavourable' technological balance of payments.

(*d*) United States direct investment abroad has played an important part in spreading new technologies abroad. This mechanism for spreading new technologies is not without its complications. The growth of United States direct investment in Europe has gone fast and far enough to create a fear that European countries have, or will, become unduly dependent on United States business. This fear may be based on the view that national independence may be more important than opulence, or on the view that there is not always an identity of interests between the invading United States firms and the invaded countries – in particular that United States direct investment may not add to the production growth potential of the country but simply change the control and the disposition of the profits.

(*e*) A case based on grounds of national independence is always difficult to appraise in rational terms. The extent of national economic independence in a relatively small country highly dependent on international trade is not very great, and the chance of successfully exploiting some of the fashionable new technologies on a purely national basis is very small. However, there may well be areas that could be exploited with greater national profit if selective controls on inward investments were developed and more positive Government action taken during the gestation period. Wherever there is good reason to believe that United States direct investment would lead to a suppression of competition there is a case for Government action. It would be unwise, however, to underestimate the difficulties of distinguishing between good and bad forms of inward investment. It does not appear that the French attempts to do this have so far proved at all successful.

It would be unwise to concentrate on controlling inward investment. A very great deal can be done in the United Kingdom (and other European countries) to change the conditions which make direct investment so profitable to United States firms. Improvement in management efficiency and an adaptation of industrial structures to the needs of modern technology would do much to stop an increase in the proportion of production controlled by United States firms. What is clear is that any extension of United States control due to feasible changes in management and industrial structure is not in the national interest.

(*f*) Changes in management and industrial structure would help to check the emigration of scientists and engineers. Many industrial R and D departments are not effective in generating profits, partly because they are too small and partly because of a maldistribution of scientists and engineers between R and D and production activities. With a reduction in the number of firms, the optimal sizes of R and D departments could be achieved at the same time as the distribution of scientific manpower was improved. Reforms here would make it possible to improve salaries, R and D facilities, and growth.

(*g*) It is not possible to make a precise measure of the balance of payments effects of inward investment. Much of the published statistical information on the details of United States direct investment relates to Western Europe generally and has not been subdivided by countries. The statistical information for oil companies is particularly unsatisfactory (as indeed it is for United Kingdom companies). My guesstimates for the United Kingdom indicate that United States direct investment in manufacturing has had a directly beneficial effect on the balance of payments. The indirect effects cannot be calculated, though my guess is that they too have been favourable. But even a generally favourable result is not proof that all inward investment – or all forms of inward investment – has a good effect. A fall off in capital inflows, a rise in the proportion of remitted profits and a greater dependence on local funds, could go far enough to tip the direct balance of advantage the other way. The United States interest equalization tax, which has retarded European use of the United States capital market and encouraged United States subsidiaries to greater reliance on the European market, has recently reduced Europe's direct balance of payments advantage from United States direct investment. A tax on the borrowing of United States subsidiaries in the United Kingdom equivalent to the United States interest equalization tax may well be in our interest – so long as the other European countries adopted the same policy. Such a tax might generate new forms of United States direct enterprise –

and in particular joint ventures with United Kingdom and other European firms. There is much to be said in favour of such a development, though here too, as was pointed out in the section on national independence, an improvement in the marketing efficiency of United Kingdom firms would produce the same result without specific Government action.

REFERENCES

1. National Science Foundation, *Reviews of Data on Science Resources*, Volume 1, No. 4 (May 1965).
2. C. FREEMAN and A. YOUNG, *The Research and Development Effort* (OECD, 1965).
3. See *Resources of Scientific and Technical Personnel in the OECD Area* (OECD, 1964); and FREEMAN and YOUNG, *op. cit.*
4. *Survey of Current Business*, Table 8 (United States Department of Commerce, September 1965).
5. *Ibid.* Direct investments are defined as investments in which United States firms or individuals have a directly held voting interest of 25% or more – a definition which covers most United States industrial investment abroad.
6. *Bundesbank Bulletin* (May 1965).
7. Estimates by National Industrial Conference Board. See *United States Production Abroad and the Balance of Payments* (1966). In 1964, 21·4% of the plant and equipment expenditure of United States manufacturing firms was in overseas subsidiaries. In mining and petroleum the percentage was 35·3.
8. For a list of United States achievements in the United Kingdom, see J. H. DUNNING, *American Investment in British Manufacturing Industry* (Allen & Unwin, 1958).
9. One of the most significant findings in the recent report on *United States Production Abroad and the Balance of Payments* by the National Industrial Conference (1966) is that many United States companies 'found that their joint-venture partners or licensees have comparatively ineffective sales organizations; consequently the United States companies increased their equity in the foreign enterprises so as to gain control of marketing'.

10. For an estimate of the value of physical assets, see J. REVELL, 'The Wealth of the Nation', *Moorgate and Wall Street* (Spring 1966).

11. The National Industrial Conference Board report *Costs and Competition: American Experience Abroad* (1961) gives information on costs of production in United States firms with overseas subsidiaries. In the respondent firms, total unit costs were reported to be lower in the United Kingdom than in the United States in 74% of the cases; the same in 13% and higher in 13%. Costs were less than 85% of United States costs in almost 55% of the cases. For the Common Market, costs were lower than in the United States in 64% of the cases, the same in 9% and higher in 27%. Costs were lower by 15% or more in 48% of the cases. It was also reported that 31% of United States firms with subsidiaries in the United Kingdom found competition less intense, compared to 19% who found it more intense.

12. See *United States Production Abroad* (ref. 9), pp. 61, 133–4.

13. Quoted in C. FREEMAN, 'Research and Development in Electronic Capital Goods', *National Institute Economic Review* (November 1965), p. 49.

14. See J. H. DUNNING, 'British Investment in United States Industry', *Moorgate and Wall Street* (Autumn 1961); and *United States Production Abroad* (ref. 9).

15. S. HIRSCH has tested the product cycle view of international competitiveness – based on the proposition that the relative importance of capital, management ability, and skilled and unskilled labour as products pass through the stages of innovation, rapid growth, and maturity – against the United States experience in electronics. Between 1960 and 1963 the United States exports of electronic products in the rapid growth phase of the cycle rose by 66% compared to 40% for mature products; imports of electronic products still in the rapid growth phase grew from 15–20% of exports, while those in the mature phase grew from 125–200% of exports. See *National Institute Economic Review* (November 1965).

16. See the Royal Society memorandum, *Emigration of Scientists and Engineers* (February 1963).

17. J. H. DUNNING, 'The Present Role of United States Investment in British Industry', *Moorgate and Wall Street* (Spring 1961).

18. *Survey of Current Business*, November 1966.

II

The Conditions of Industrial Innovation*

I. INVENTION AND INNOVATION

Innovation is the setting up of a new production function. To get its nature clear we need to distinguish it from *invention*. Invention is the creation of a new idea or technique. The innovation is the application of that new idea or technique to the actual processes of production. This process of application often requires a lengthy and expensive period of *development*. This is well recognized in the terminology of industrial research establishments. They refer to R and D or, in engineering, to design and development.

The distinction between invention and innovation is clearly made in such well-known books as Paul Mantoux's *The Industrial Revolution in the Eighteenth Century* and in Schumpeter's *Business Cycles*. A few recent examples from *Industry and Technical Progress* by Carter and Williams will suffice here:

(*a*) The transfer machine was invented in 1923 and tried out in the Morris works at Coventry. This full-scale trial showed that the ancillary control equipment was unreliable. When twenty years later the ancillary equipment had become reliable, transfer machines were coaxed into use by the shortage of machinists – the invention became an innovation.

(*b*) Penicillin as an anti-bacterial substance was first observed by Fleming in 1928. As an unstable substance (and therefore difficult to manipulate chemically), it was thought not to have practical value in medicine. In other words, the 'invention' was not expected to lead to an innovation. However, owing to the systematic researches of Chain and Florey between 1938 and 1940, and to the developments in chemotherapy associated with the introduction of sulphonomides, the medical promise of penicillin was realized.

* Lecture given at Institut d'Administration des Entreprises, Université D'Aix-Marseille, on 19th January, 1959.

The possibility of innovation now depended on inventing methods of production suitable for commercial production. This problem of scaling up was, with Florey's active co-operation, solved in the United States in 1942, fourteen years after Fleming first isolated penicillin. The substantial innovation was then possible.

(c) Whittle filed his first patent on the idea of combining a gas turbine with jet propulsion in 1929. In 1937 an actual jet engine had its first, and partly satisfactory, test run. By 1940 improvements in design and materials were such that a reliable jet engine existed. That is to say it had been invented. It was, however, another four or five years before the problems of development – the re-design of the engine to make economical production possible – were solved. This process of development like so many others was very expensive and entailed a process differing widely from the original inventing process.

If a company attempts to innovate on the basis of incomplete or defective development the cost of the subsequent premature innovation may be tremendous. A good, though tragic case of this is the original Comet jet airliner. At the time the R and D involved was thought to be a model of its kind. In fact there was insufficient technical and theoretical knowledge about fatigue in structures.

Often development costs many times the cost of the invention. For example, it is expected that the cost of developing TSR-2 with its new turbo-jet engine will be about £20,000,000. Furthermore, the actual innovation requires an investment in productive equipment. Some idea of the significance of this is given by the calculation of some chemical companies for a planned innovation, namely, 10% for research, 25% for development, and 65% for factory cost. The planning and financial implications of this will be considered later.

Of course not all inventions lead to innovation. Only a small proportion of scientific or engineering ideas thought worthy of further industrial research are then thought worthy of the often costly process of development, and only a proportion of the ideas taken for development are actually embodied in new processes or new products. Some ideas not taken past the development stage now may be turned into innovations later, because of a direct improvement in the invention or an indirect improvement in ancillary processes. This happened, for example, with such different things as penicillin and transfer machines; it may happen with the new *chemical* process for making steel developed by the British Iron and Steel Research

Association. The fact that the practical success of particular R and D projects is in some measure unpredictable sets some very interesting and difficult problems – that will be taken up later – in planning R and D.

2. INDUCING INNOVATIONS

Over a large section of industry – in fact in the industries based on science – innovation is an organized process. In these industries there are chance discoveries and there are discoveries brought to the industry from outside. The main discoveries, however, are engineered by the firms in the industry. Just as firms incur selling expenses to improve conditions of demand, so firms incur development expenses to improve conditions of supply by getting attractive new products or more efficient processes. Innovation does not simply come from outside the economic system – it is created within it. Even many of the inventions on which the innovations are based are created within the economic system in the hope that innovations will come from them.

The extent of planned innovation within industry is in considerable measure reflected in the following figures (see page 36).

It will be seen from this table that there is a fairly close relation between the employment of scientists and engineers in R and D and in manufacture except in aircraft and precision instruments (where, after development, the production process depends on engineering craftsmen), other manufacturing (a miscellaneous collection) and constructional engineering and railway equipment (where there is much *ad hoc* development work in the manufacturing process).

The main explanation of these differences is that some industries are based on science, while others are not. We find the greatest attention to R and D where a developed science or technology has a close bearing on the industry's products of processes, for then a discovery in the appropriate science may have an immediate or large effect on the firms in the industry. Furthermore, where an industry is based on science there will be a vast amount of relevant scientific knowledge, as well as, coming from the normal processes of higher education, a supply of scientists capable of using that science to improve processes or products.

Those industries whose technology is based on art rather than science give less attention to R and D. Immediately at least, science has less to offer. Where the sciences underlying a

technology are not in an advanced state, applied research must be on
a trial and error basis. By contrast with a science-based industry few
ideas can be 'tried out on paper', most must be tried out in experiments and pilot models. In consequence, applied research is less
productive for a given expenditure on it.

Industrial group	Number of qualified scientists and engineers, as proportion of total employment, in:	
	Research and development	Manufacture and other work
Mineral oil refining	1·84	3·40
Aircraft	1·49	0·40
Chemicals and allied trades	1·27	1·40
Electrical engineering	1·18	0·86
Rayon, nylon, etc.	0·61	0·48
Precision instruments, etc.	0·56	0·30
Non-ferrous metals	0·32	0·76
Other plant and machinery	0·29	0·68
Other manufacturing	0·24	0·32
Constructional engineering	0·17	1·30
Motor vehicles, etc.	0·16	0·26
Iron and steel	0·12	0·38
Bricks, china, glass, cement	0·11	0·22
Other metal goods	0·09	0·41
Food, drink, tobacco	0·08	0·23
Wood, cork, paper, printing	0·07	0·10
Other textiles and leather	0·07	0·25
Shipbuilding and marine engineering	0·03	0·33
Agricultural machinery	0·03	0·34
Cotton	0·03	0·05
Railway equipment	0·02	0·41
Wool textiles	0·02	0·06
Clothing	0·003	0·012

Source: Command Paper 902, HMSO.

A low yield to expenditure on applied research in empirical
industries is frequently reinforced by lack of interest in science or by
inability to use what science could contribute. Both these things
result when the number of scientists and technologists employed is
small. For then both the knowledge of what science can do to change
technology and the capacity to adapt outside technological developments to the particular needs of the industry are small. Very few
developments even in applied science have a very direct or simple
application to technology. Thus even when a research association

communicates the results of its applied research to member firms, many firms are unable to use the results (unless embodied in a purchasable gadget) because they need interpretation and further development work.

As the technological base of an industry is shifted from the empirical towards the scientific, the productivity and profitability of R and D increases. With the expansion of fundamental and background applied research in the older established industries the interest in applied R and D has increased. This is one reason why industrial R and D has increased and why we may expect it to increase still further.

The percentage employment of scientists in R and D is not necessarily a good guide to innovation. Thus, as can be seen from the table, some industries do little R and D but do employ a significant number of highly trained scientists and engineers in production departments. These may do *ad hoc* development work, particularly by way of adapting innovations in other industries for their own use. Furthermore, some industries by their nature tend to be dependent on other industries for their innovations, or at least for many of them. Thus outside the chemical industry many users of chemicals naturally rely on the chemical firms to develop new chemicals and to demonstrate their qualities and uses; most users of machine tools rely on makers for ready-made innovations; mere assemblers of components, as, for example, some motor-car firms, may be expected to rely on suppliers to do the metallurgical, electrical or engineering R and D leading to new metals or presses or transmission systems.

Planned inventions and innovations in one industry often create unplanned innovations in other industries, or at least create the opportunity for them. In *Industry and Technical Progress*, Carter and I called this the *gate effect* – it opens gates to technical change. Sometimes these planned inventions and innovations may be said to trigger off changes in other industries. The existence of this *trigger effect* depends on two things: (i) the possibility of combining the externally acquired new knowledge or techniques with existing internal knowledge or techniques – as in, for example, many applications of automatic controls to processes or machine operations – and (ii) the willingness and capacity of firms to use these externally created opportunities.

Whether we look at the matter from the standpoint of industries in the first or the second half of the table, relations between firms are very important. One can think of any firm in three senses: firstly, as a customer of other firms; secondly, as a supplier of other firms; and, thirdly, as a competitor or potential competitor with other firms. What any firm can do or is pressed to do in the field of innovation will depend very largely on what sort of help or stimulus it gets from its customers, its suppliers, and its competitors, and it is this *chain of relations* between firms that plays in many ways a dominating part in the speed or the slowness with which firms in any country apply science to industry.

3. THE ECONOMICS OF INNOVATION

The economics of innovation are of varying degrees of complexity. I will distinguish three main cases: (i) a new machine or process that has been through the development stage; (ii) a new product at a similar stage of development; (iii) expenditure on research or development in the hope that it will lead to new products and processes.

In the first case – the question of whether or not to install a new method of production – the issue is often apparently easy. The cost of the installation will be known and (let us assume) the effect on cost per unit output can be calculated. From this and an estimate of the life of the new machine or process the yield on the capital investment can be calculated. Yet there are many examples of seemingly profitable new methods that do not take on, or take on slowly. Why so? Is it that businessmen are irrational or slothful or unable to get finance?

There are sometimes certain practical difficulties about innovation that often complicate the issues. The first is the problem of assessing the potential benefit of the new method. If the firm lacks a costing system it cannot judge the relative profitability of the new and the old. Or, if, because the technology of an industry has been based on art rather than science, a firm does not employ scientists and engineers, it may not be in a position to assess the cost implications of the new technique. In *Industry and Technical Progress*, we gave many examples of this difficulty. What will count with such firms will be the proof that firms which have pioneered the new methods are prospering.

A further complication may be the *operation* of the new method – it may require the recruitment of scientists and engineers, which in turn may require a radical change in management methods and salary scales. The 'Urwick Gap' between personal management and functional management may make unreal our first financial calculation of yield.[1]

The third complication is finance, which an innovation may require. In Britain the new issue market is not suitable for issues smaller than £50,000 or for companies with assets smaller than £100,000. Although institutions like ICFC exist to nurse small companies through awkward growth stages there is often ignorance of what finance is available or great fear of getting into debt or of losing control.

These complications increase if the new method (i) has not been fully proved (as in many cases it cannot be until it is put into full operation) or (ii) entails a significant change in scale of production and therefore an estimate of elasticity of demand. In these cases the problematic nature of the potential benefit will generally appear more significant the greater the technical ignorance of the decision takers and the less their competence and confidence in market research. Presumably, also the prospect of yield if things go well will need to be higher to induce any firms to take the risk of what might be a premature innovation.

These complications, which are mostly problems of adapting organizations to new conditions, are often screened by rough monetary calculations of prospective yields. It is important not to screen them. The real barriers to innovation are, as Professor Carter and I have shown, often more important than finance.

In the second case – that of a new product – the complications may be even greater. They will be if the new product is not simply an improvement on an existing product, designed to strengthen the competitive position by meeting a known need, but something radically new. Sometimes – whatever the preliminary market research may have shown – the introduction of a new product must be very speculative. This is most likely where a firm cannot 'creep up on a problem' by starting a small-scale plant but must for technical reasons start with a large-scale plant. Here the question of what prospective yield on capital makes an investment rational becomes quite difficult.

In *Investment in Innovation*, Carter and I give evidence of the relation between actual and expected yields. In our sample the correlation was very low (0·13), and in general we found that over-estimation and under-estimation were equally likely. Since for firms with several innovations the gains tended to balance the losses, they could reasonably set a lower figure for acceptable prospective yield than firms with fewer innovations.

The most difficult problem in innovation economics is where firms invest in creating the materials for their own innovation.

For a clear understanding of what research can contribute the research possibilities must be related to the technological management and financial resources of the firm. Research that is paid for but not utilized is so much loss to the firm. If research is treated in isolation from the production problems and from the financial and human resources of the firm, only loss is likely to result, because the research output will be most irrelevant. Equally, if the research department is treated as just another production department, to be run on well-known principles of production engineering, there is not likely to be a worthwhile research output.

To say what research can contribute requires a knowledge of science on the one hand, and of the technological and the management problems of the firm on the other. It is useless to create a new product for which there is no market, or a new process that for economical working requires an output in excess of market needs, or a new product that requires a capital outlay or a production technique well beyond the capacity of the firm. It is equally useless for a non-scientist to choose problems for research, simply because a solution to them would make the greatest contribution to an increase of profit or financial stability. Problems so chosen may be scientifically unpromising.

It follows that advice on 'what research can do for the firm' should only be given by a competent scientist with a knowledge and appreciation of the production, selling, and financial problems of the firm, or, where such a scientist does not exist, by two or more people who can between them judge the possibilities of useful researches on this or that line, as well as their potential commercial significance.

The appropriate procedure is to compile a list of worthwhile R and D projects. This list, which would result from suggestions by and discussions between research, production and sales departments, will be based on *research economics*; that is to say, the problems would be those judged to be both capable of scientific solution *and* commercially significant.

The list will have certain implications for the finance, research, personnel, management, and sales departments. The next step is to state those implications. A rough calculation can be made of the financial implications of the programme – the direct cost of the

RandD and (even more roughly) the consequential financial cost of new plant and equipment if the research is successful. The implications for RandD personnel can also be roughed out. How far could the programme be managed by existing persons, and over what period of time?

Innovation requires to be *managed* into being. A guess can be made from past experience about the proportion of RandD projects likely to be successful. This will give some idea of the management implications of the programme. What rate of innovation would have to be managed? How difficult would the management of this innovation be: would it require new divisions of the company, would teething troubles be great, would co-operation from other firms be involved, what sort of sales promotion problems would it present to the sales department?

With this information, based it is true on very rough calculations, it becomes possible to make a judgement on the list of worthwhile problems.

Suppose the direct financial cost is 15% of turnover. This cost can then be set against the financial resources of the company and alongside the other claims for finance – such as finance for stocks and work-in-progress, sales organization, building, replacement of existing equipment, reserves, financial investments, etc. It may quickly be obvious that at most 3% of turnover can be allocated to new developments after all other necessary commitments are met (assuming present production, prices and dividends). What then of the remaining competition for funds between research, sales, re-equipment? Rough estimates of the return from more investment in research, as compared with more investment in such things as new machines, then enable a decision to be taken – provided a decision has first been made about the period of time for which the firm is prepared to wait for a return. Thus it may have to choose between a fairly certain 10% yield in the next five years from the purchase of new machines or (after a wait of two or three years) a possible return of 30% per annum from investment in research. No formula will help a firm to make a right choice of this kind. The decision should, however, be tilted towards investment in research the more likely it is that such investment, undertaken now, will help to offset a probable increase in competition in the near future.

Suppose a limit of 3% is set on financial grounds. This does not in itself create a case for the expenditure of that amount. If such a programme requires a significant addition to the RandD depart-

D

ments, next it must be asked how fast these departments can be built up without loss of efficiency. It is seldom possible to increase R and D effort quickly and efficiently.

Finally, a judgement must be made about the likelihood of successful R and D presenting projects beyond the capacity of the firm to use. If it is clear that there is likely to be excess supply the programme should be reduced.

Judgement on these last two matters requires the same combination of knowledge about industrial research and about management as does the definition of the potentialities of research. The board can only make this judgement if it is properly briefed and if it is capable of appreciating the brief. This means that the firm needs a board with an appropriate range of scientific, managerial, and financial skills, as well as a research department that has a well-developed 'cost-consciousness'.

If a firm is not just starting R and D, it will be sufficient on many occasions simply to examine carefully *the excluded projects*. With these, what is the probability of success; over what period of time? How profitable would a new product of process based on them be? Even so, it is wise periodically to make a full list of the research possibilities. This helps to prevent the omission of important problems, for it is natural to check research in progress against this list of projects.

By such procedures it becomes possible to make reasonable 'guesstimates' of the best level of investment in development.

4. SUMMARY OF THE CONDITIONS OF RAPID INNOVATION

In my examination of innovation in various industries I have found it useful to divide the problem into:

(*a*) The opportunities to innovate.
(*b*) The capacity to innovate.
(*c*) The pressures to innovate.

(*a*) *Opportunities* to innovate come, in descending order of remoteness, from: (i) the advance of science; (ii) planned development from the basis of existing scientific knowledge; and (iii) innovations in other industries.

The advance of science depends on a country's system of education. Industrial R and D also depends on education because of the need for scientists and engineers. It also depends on an operational approach to industrial R and D. If development is to be successful it cannot be added to a firm like an outboard motor to a boat; it must be treated as one of a group of closely related management techniques.[2]

There is a special problem of creating opportunities to innovate in traditional industries. There because the sciences underlying the technology are not in an advanced state, R and D is not immediately profitable. Because it is not, these industries tend to stay technically stagnant and there tends to be a drain of talent away from these industries. In such industries – if market prospects are good – it may be wise for the State (as in the case of research associations in the United Kingdom to encourage the growth of background research in an effort to shift the basis of technology from art to science. Once this happens the productivity and profitability of applied R and D will increase: the self-perpetuating nature of stagnancy will then be checked.

Each country would be well advised to have a high-powered *committee on research economics* to identify research problems that look promising both on economic and scientific grounds. It may be, for example, that given their importance to practically all industries and the promise of research into them, research-development expenditure on steel, machine tools, and control systems is much too low and/or short term. The chain effects of successful research here could be tremendous.

(*b*) *The capacity* to use opportunities to innovate depends on finance, personnel, and organization. Finance must set some limits to innovation: the supply of savings is not unlimited. Except for small and new firms, however, in post-war United Kingdom the limit has not been set by finance, but by personnel. There has been a critical shortage of scientists and engineers which has affected not only the process of development, but also the introduction of new techniques. To close the development gap requires scientists and engineers not only in development departments but also in production and sales departments. Many new techniques require scientists/technologists to run them or to develop their market potential through 'technical selling'.

The conduct of a firm entails the exercise of a number of functions represented by the division between the board and the management, and by the division of management into functions such as production, sales, finance, control, development, and personnel. Decisions on what to produce and how to produce it must be made, and then executed. The function of execution entails a set of authority relations running from the managing director to the foremen or charge-hands. Also of course it entails more than a set of authority relations. For various decisions are made at different levels in the authority structure. Some decisions are deliberately left for lower levels of management – particularly details of technique – others are made necessary by unforeseen events or difficulties during the process of execution. Managers, therefore, require technical and social skills to enable them to give effect to policy decisions and executive directions. The call on technical or technological skills of managers – to enable the formulation of correct decisions about policy and execution – becomes greater as the extent and frequency of innovation increases. In a craft or traditional industry the working craftsman can decide most problems of execution within departments, but as science is applied to industry dependence on functional specialists must increase.

The process of rational decision-making – both at the level of policy and at the level of execution – also becomes increasingly dependent on specialists who perform the functions of investigation and evaluation. (RandD are aspects of these functions.) In the performance of these functions the dependence on formal organization is reduced relative to the dependence on the scientific or technical skills of the functionaries. In turn, these functionaries cannot function within a rigid and formal authority structure. Informal or *ad hoc* relations between the people performing the functions of investigation, evaluation, decision taking, and execution become essential to efficiency. By its very nature the authority structure must often become inappropriate or irrelevant to the process of technical change.

In many cases the use of an invention involves a significant change in the organization of the firm. Thus it may be necessary to introduce into the firm functional specialists who disrupt the old principles or practices of line management. This disruption may create resistance to change by departmental managers and foremen. To overcome this it may be necessary to think out new lines of responsibility and new spheres of influence; or to change the men who hold particular management positions. All people who have worked in this field could quote cases of resistance to change, or difficulties in carrying through change that results from failures to adapt the organization and the balance of skills in the firm to the new technical situation.

(*c*) *The pressures* to innovate come from outside firms and, in certain cases, from inside firms.

The main outside pressure is competition. All I want to say here about this is that we need to give more attention to the *conditions of effective competition* – effective in the sense that encourages innovation. Competition *per se* does not encourage innovation because it does nothing to create the opportunities to innovate, and sometimes through depressing profits and prospects reduces the capacity to innovate. *Once, however, in the industry concerned there is ample provision for education and research* the competitive pressure to innovate can encourage not only innovation but also investment in invention.[3]

Given competition in this type of situation (which may have to be created by Government action on education and research) the number of firms is not nearly so important as is often argued. Competition between few firms may be intense. This may be so, even though there is often little open price competition between them. Competition based on quality and the creation of new products is often much more important than open price competition. (I say open price competition here because frequently economies of innovation are passed on to consumers by letting prices fall *relative* to factor prices.)

Perhaps we think too much in terms of trivial textbook examples of product differentiation, such as brands of soap, cosmetics, and breakfast foods, and too little in terms of new products and processes and continual improvement in their reliability and performance: think of gramophone, television, radar, aircraft, artificial fibres, drugs, plastics, and metals.

Intense competition even between the few is made more certain where there are many opportunities to innovate. This happens because of the growing number of alternative ways of providing for particular wants. Building materials provide a good example. In such a situation, to count the number of firms in an industry may be pretty useless: the main competitors may be outside the industry. The pressure of competition increases when one's potential competitors are unidentifiable: when competition is both direct and indirect.

In addition, and this is my final point, where both opportunities and capacities to innovate are created through the organization of industrial R and D there will be an internal pressure to innovate.

For the scientists and engineers employed in RandD will have an *interest* in creating new processes and products. Their pay and their prestige will depend on 'getting science used'. Any firm that creates a RandD department is in effect creating a *pressure group* within itself, and this group will press for innovations.

REFERENCES

1. For one such case see my chapter, 'The Pottery Industry', *The Structure of British Industry*, edited by D. BURN (Cambridge University Press, 1958).
2. C. F. CARTER and B. R. WILLIAMS, *Industry and Technical Progress*, Chapters 6, 7, 12, 16 (Oxford University Press, 1957).
3. I have given case examples of this in my chapters on pottery and building materials, *The Structure of British Industry* (see ref. 1).

III

The Evaluation of Industrial Research*

There is a limit to the resources – men and money – available for industrial research. Evaluation of the results of industrial research is thus important for two reasons: first, in an attempt to establish the optimum expenditure of effort in R and D; second, in an attempt to ensure the best use of those resources that are available.

We may value scientific research from the standpoint of the firm, or from the standpoint of the industry, or from the standpoint of society with its interest in tradition and stability, or from the standpoint of the community with its interest in material wealth.

I. THE VALUATION OF RESEARCH BY THE FIRM

Industrial research is not cultivated for its intrinsic worth but for the results it will bring in production. As it devises means for the achievement of certain ends it is rational only if it is economic. It should therefore 'pay for itself' from economies in process improvements or out of the profits of new products. For the United Kingdom we have very little information about the profits firms derive from industrial research, and, as already mentioned, many firms do not draw up a profit and loss account for their research activities.

What evidence then is there that applied research is worthwhile – that it pays. Some firms can provide this. The position from the standpoint of the economy as a whole will be mentioned in the final section of this paper. The more significant question – how much pays most? – cannot be answered by the vast majority of firms.

The evidence relating to whether research pays or not is historical. A research profit and loss account would often have to cover different time periods. On the debit side would appear total spending on research for a particular time period, while on the credit side would

* Paper written for the European Productivity Agency Conference on the Rational Organization of Industrial Research, April 1956.

appear profits or notional profits accruing from this past expenditure, less actual or imputed interest on the capital expenditure involved. The credit side in the case of new products would cover the profits earned, and in the case of the new process the difference between the operating costs of the new process and the old. In this latter case the profits might be 'notional' in that part of the 'profit' may have been shared with the workers and the consumers. But unless the firm has a monopoly, it is reasonable to include this notional profit on the credit side, as in the absence of the process improvement the competitive position of the firm would have suffered. Where, however, a process improvement involves an increase in scale of output, some adjustment must be made for the consequential lowering of price. Revenue from licences, less any consequential cross-licensing payments, would also appear on the credit side, as well as any savings on licences that resulted from product or process improvement.

The time lag between the dates in the debit and credit columns is significant in three senses. First, in the case of many companies just starting R and D, there are likely to be quick and large returns to be gained from immediate production problems. As these are solved, the chance for quick returns will be reduced and the planning period will have to lengthen. Second, perhaps through no fault of the research people, successes and failures may cluster in particular periods and when there is a cluster of successes application of some will be delayed. Third, some projects may take a long time to get into full production. For example, if we drew up a profit and loss account for atomic energy now it would doubtless look rather alarming! A research profit and loss account can only act as a guide to present policy. Future needs will be different from past needs and the theoretical evaluation of technical and economic possibilities will have to be made in each period.

The time for which firms can afford to wait for returns is partly a function of available capital resources. Not many firms could afford to copy Dupont, who induced Dr Carothers to come from Harvard and continue his work on high polymers – work which after ten years led to the manufacture of nylon; or the Badische Anilin-und-Soda Fabrik which spent fifteen years and nearly £2,000,000 in 'patient money' before they learned how to make synthetic indigo. Often what might be called fundamental industrial research leads to very profitable results but it is generally expensive and, perhaps more important, so unpredictable as to the time of result that only companies with a very large capital can afford to gamble with it.

Given the average time for which firms can wait for financial returns from research the extent to which research results are used should be carefully considered. Non-utilization of research results is a sign of wasted effort and expenditure. Some of this waste is unavoidable in that the research is well chosen but, in the result, fruitless. Avoidable waste occurs when the research is badly chosen – as when the time scale is wrong for the firm; or when the potential profits from application are too small. Avoidable waste occurs also when usable research results are not used. This may occur when the results are poured out at a rate that is excessive in relation to the potential capital growth of the firm. In this case, the research effort is excessive. On the other hand the results may not be used because the management is inefficient. In certain cases, however, making the management efficient will involve a transfer of staff from research to production or sales, and this may involve a reduction in research, for a time at least (a time which, when scientists are in short supply, may be long). What I have been saying about research in relation to production can also be said, without much change, for relations within 'industrial research', between R and D.

The research *output* is properly regarded as a production *input*. Without a close relation between the research, production, and sales department, the appropriate relation between these outputs and inputs is unlikely to be achieved. The significant thing here, however, is that this type of output-input accounting should be used in addition to financial accounting as it can reveal misdirection that one or two profitable projects may obscure.

Where the time-horizon of the firm is longer, output-input accounting becomes vaguer. For then 'fundamental' applied research may be used with three objects in mind. First, there may be a need for theoretical work in the firm's field of interest, theoretical work not carried out in universities or research associations. Second, one big success from long-term research may pay for the research department for years. Examples of this could be drawn from many big concerns such as Metro-Vick, and the Bell Telephone Company. Third, the reputation of the research laboratories at universities may be a great aid in recruitment. Young scientists with a yearning for 'fundamental' work may turn naturally to applied research or production as they come to learn of the interesting problems. Further, the research department may be used as a recruiting ground by the production and sales departments. In so far as this happens, it should be easier to get research results through quickly. These cases extend the area over which a broad judgement must be exercised, and increase the difficulty of using both the financial and the output-input methods of accounting. That is not to say that such methods of accounting are useless. They are not. Where so much is unpredictable a few firm facts are an indispensable aid to the exercise of judgement.

According to Mr Mark Spade: 'It is not absolutely necessary to have a research department – at least not one of your own. In fact, probably the most efficient and economical type of research is to have an employee whom you can really *trust* working in the research department of your principal competitor.' Not many firms are in this happy position of trust, still fewer in the happy position of employing such a fellow with the capacity to bring back all the 'knowhow' free of patent difficulties! There are nevertheless some firms that will get greater profit from purchasing licenses and from relying on the technical advice of suppliers than from running their own research. This may reduce an unnecessary duplication of research effort. Greater attention to estimating the return from research would enable us to make a better judgement on the profit limits of parasitism.

2. EVALUATION FROM THE STANDPOINT OF THE INDUSTRY

What is not waste from the standpoint of the firm may be waste from the standpoint of the 'industry', if I may use such a fiction. More important, what is not feasible for any firm may be important for the industry.

The extent to which much the same industrial research is done many times over is not known. There must, however, be considerable duplication of effort. Some of this must be regarded as an indispensable concomitant of competition, though how much of it is so is unknown. When scientists are in short supply it is important to look for economies of effort here. Is it not possible to list a set of applied research problems of interest to all the firms and have these pre-development problems solved and available for the whole industry? To a certain extent this is done by the research associations, but I do not know of any analysis of the extent to which this is done. Another factor of importance in the 'industry' interest would be the publication of 'failed' research efforts. This would help to reduce a duplication of wasted effort.

There are some problems that are not profitable for any one firm to solve, although the solution would be profitable for the whole industry. This is so in industries where the typical size of firm is small, but cases can also be found in industries where the typical size of firm is large. Research associations have an important role here too, as have also Government research or development contracts.

This type of 'industry' research is extremely difficult to evaluate. How should, for example, the extent of public grant to research associations be determined? If there is no applied research in firms in the industry, the judgement could be made after the fashion outlined in the previous section. But if this is the situation the work of the research associations is not likely to be very productive. For research associations are not near enough to the production problem to do the development work efficiently. But, if firms are not able to appreciate and develop the research association output, it would be unwise to conclude that the research work is necessarily excessive. It may be preparing the way for a change of management methods in the industry. But under these conditions, the question whether the research association has paid sufficient attention to the mechanism of technical change and arranged its research programme with this in mind is relevant. Asking this question may lead to a change in the direction of effort.

Where firms in the industry do conduct research the judgement of the effectiveness of research association effort would have, presumably, to be based on an examination of the extent to which the research association output became inputs in the research, development, or production departments of firms. The usual qualifications about management apply here too.

A large industry may sometimes be able to make research possible in a smaller industry. In this case, which is similar to Government development contracts in the defence sphere, a large industry may take part of the risk of R and D by placing contracts. The larger industry or firm recognizes its interest in the R and D of another industry and makes possible development that would not otherwise take place. There are no special problems from the standpoint of the industry in evaluating research of this kind. The main problem is why more of it is not done.

3. EVALUATION FROM THE 'NON-MONETARY' STANDPOINT OF THE SOCIETY

The society has an interest in things other than material wealth. This is obvious, but as we often overlook the obvious we need occasionally to remind ourselves of it. Much of the talk and thought about the lag in the application of science to industry implies that we have a clear duty to overcome these lags – implies in other words that society has a duty to change all habits, attitudes, forms of education and of organization that stand in the way. Society has such a clear duty only if its primary value or objective is to achieve the degree of technological change that maximizes material wealth. I do not believe that this is the primary objective of any society though the ruling party in Russia gives the impression at times that it is trying to create such a society.

Technological change does have a profound impact on society. Indeed unless society's other interests have the power of expression, technological change made in the interests of material wealth may become the dominating objective. This happened in the United Kingdom in the last century. This industrial revolution was not, however, based on industrial research, and in the United Kingdom at least the scientists grew in 'purity' as the nineteenth-century industrial revolution advanced.

Now that industrial research is an important activity of both Government and industry, it is wise to get clear the nature of society's interest in it. This interest is two-fold – in the scale of the research and in the objectives of the research.

Assuming that the industrial research is conducted with a reasonable degree of efficiency – i.e. that both the preliminary appraisal of potentialities and the conduct of the R and D is efficient – society has an interest in the scale of research because it has an interest in the rate of industrial change. The greater the pace of change the more difficult is it to make satisfactory changes in the patterns of living. I will not say anything further on this for I believe that in the United Kingdom the rate of change is still below the level at which comfortable changes in society can be made. In any case, as I will argue in the next section, in the British situation the area of choice is probably small.

Society also has an interest in the objectives of research. It is often asserted that the application of science to industry must lead to an increase in large-scale organization and so to the gradual elimination of small firms. Technical processes in some industries (e.g. heavy chemicals) or sections of industries (e.g. *assembly* of motor cars) do lend support to this generalization. But there are many technical developments which do not. However, the average cost of research per fully qualified graduate worker in industry, including his assistants, is about £3,000 a year. At this cost many firms are too small to afford a useful R and D department. This means that industrial research is concentrated in the larger firms. This almost inevitably slants the goals of research effort towards the creation of technological solutions that fit in with the needs of large-scale organization. The existence of research associations and development engineers provides some safeguard against this distortion of applied research but my suspicion is that the safeguard is insufficient. It is not easy to find the number of researchers employed by the different kinds of employers. The Census of Production for 1948 gives a figure of 30,000 research workers in industry, but this includes an unknown number of 'unqualified' scientists and technicians. Even so, the figure must be very substantially higher than the 1,450 graduate scientists working in research associations. Nor do research associations cater only for small firms.

If I am right in thinking that the goals of research effort are in some part a function of the size of the industrial organizations, conducting the applied research, then a good deal of further thought and enquiry should be given to the organization of R and D. For, clearly, society's interest in the scale of research effort is not independent of its interest in the impact of research on the size of firm.

4. EVALUATION FROM THE 'MONETARY' STANDPOINT OF SOCIETY

When output per head increases, the increase can be used to expand leisure or the supply of goods. Advanced industrial communities take more of the increased production potential in goods than in leisure. This division between the two may be taken as a rough index of society's desire for higher material standards of living. Any society that sanctions competition within the law also displays a desire for higher material standards of living. This last element is most important when a country is dependent on competitive international trade. For then the capacity to control the pace of technical change in the interests of stability and easy transition is limited by the pace of technical change in competitor nations.

Competitive strength in international trade may depend on factors that individual firms or industries are unable to influence. This is obvious in the case of monetary or fiscal policy. It is obvious also in the case of education in science and technology. Yet the scale of education sets the ultimate limit to industrial research.

In 1914 industrial research was rare. During the First World

War the Government was faced with the need to ensure a greater application of science in industry and amongst other actions created the Department of Scientific and Industrial Research. Industrial research increased between the wars, but the big expansion has taken place since 1940. Whereas R and D expenditure in 1939 was less than 0·3% of GNP, it is now, if we include Government as well as industrial, about 1·7% of GNP. In the United States R and D expenditure was only 0·6% of GNP in 1939, but by 1955 it had also grown to about 1·7% of GNP.

If the quantitative effort in this country were to equal that in the United States, its R and D percentage would have to be considerably higher to make up for the smaller population and (after adjustment for the higher cost of research in the United States) the lower level of output per head. In other words, the United Kingdom R and D percentage would have to be increased from under 2% to over 6% of GNP, at a time when there is already a considerable shortage of scientists and engineers.

Such rough calculations are important in helping us both to keep a sense of the possible and to estimate the likely effect of a greater R and D effort. The much higher output of scientists per head in the United States should not be taken to mean that they are placing a much higher percentage of their population in R and D. But they are using scientists in production and sales to a far greater extent than the United Kingdom. How far is the apparently greater application of science to industry due to that?

In an attempt to estimate what more could be achieved from industrial research, I would therefore raise the following questions:

(*a*) Would we get a greater utilization of industrial R and D if we used a smaller proportion of our scientists in research and a greater proportion in production? or

(*b*) Are there certain key shortages of, for example, engineers, which hold up both development and the application in production? In other words, have we got a critical lack of balance in our supply of scientists?

(*c*) How important is the quantitative difference in research expenditure between the United Kingdom and the United States? Is this something that is cancelled out because spread over a larger number of firms, or are there certain national economies of scale such that we in common with Western Europe will be kept at a competitive disadvantage unless we create a European economic union? If the latter,

(*d*) Should we restrict the field of industrial R and D and concentrate on a range of problems such as nuclear energy, aircraft, and electronics? Are we, as in the political sphere, trying to do too much in too short a space of time?

I don't think any sane person would give a confident answer to any of these questions, excepting the second. Yet for an appraisal of industrial research we need the answers. Fortunately there is now a much keener interest in such questions and before long we may have some worthwhile evidence. But our society may find that the answers will not point to any simple remedial action. I will illustrate this in relation to my first question. Suppose it is true that we could get a more rapid industrial application of science if a greater proportion of our scientists were used in production. This may mean that if there were a greater industrial application more scientists would be needed in production, or that the present lack of scientists in production is holding up the application, so wasting the efforts of research scientists. If the latter, the lack of balance may be due to the failure of a firm with a research department to change its structure of organization – it is easier to tack on research as an extra department than it is to create a new organization capable of getting rapid changes in production – or it may be due to the complete absence of scientists in a different firm which could, with profit, use a new product or process. In other words, an apparently undue proportion of scientists in research *may* be a sign not that the number of research workers is excessive, but that management is wrong somewhere. To reduce industrial research in these conditions might not increase the use of scientists in production; it might simply take away the very force that would ultimately change the management of production.

Although I have called this section 'evaluation from the "monetary" standpoint of society' I have said nothing about monetary evaluation.

Can we make a monetary evaluation of the results of industrial research? This is difficult, but worth trying.

The difficulty is this. If industrial research is worthwhile it will bring an increase in national income. But it will bring an increase with a time lag. We cannot say, with the information at our disposal, what that time lag is. Further, although in the United States there are usable statistics on research development expenditure from 1920, in this country there are not. There is another difficulty, that in industrial countries national income increased substantially before there was anything we could properly call industrial R and D. Thus in the United Kingdom from 1881 to 1890 income per head, at constant prices, increased over 20%. Estimates such as this are complicated by a number of factors, such as levels of employment, changes in the terms of trade, and the exploitation of new territories. It is clear, nevertheless, that we cannot treat all increases in output per head as the consequence of applied research. This point is still more obvious in the case of Russia in the past twenty years. However, apart from growth entailing the application of known techniques in underdeveloped territories, the investment opportunity is likely to depend more and more on industrial research. The opportunity for simple inventiveness is not likely to disappear but its importance in creating investment opportunity has fallen progressively in advanced countries.

In the United States the annual increase in productivity was: 1·25% from 1910–20; 1·82% from 1920–30; 2·82% from 1930–40; 2·65% from 1940–50; and 3% from 1946–53. How much of this increase should be imputed to applied research is, at the moment, 'anyone's guess'. Thus, if we take a growth of 2·75% as representing recent United States achievement and deduct, say, 1·25% for growth due to factors such as simple inventiveness, social invention in organization, and better technical education, we get a figure of 1·5% growth due to, or rather, made possible by, applied research. This leads to an increase in income considerably greater than spending on industrial R and D even at its present level of about 1%. Research has been growing at 10% per annum – a faster rate than output per head – but on present assumed trends it would take some time before this growth in industrial R and D led to excessive expenditure on it.

This sort of calculation, however, should be treated with considerable care. In the first place the growth in national income due to other factors is a complete guess. In the second place, the appropriate time lag is unknown. In the third place, the impact of applied research on output depends on investment and there is a limit to the proportion of resources that any country is willing and able to put into investment. It may be that the answer to the question 'how much is too much?' will be 'when more investment opportunities are created than there are savings to finance them' or 'when investment opportunities are created at a rate greater than the capacity of human organization to manage innovation'.

IV

Assessing the Economics of Innovation*

There is widespread belief that the speed of industrial innovation is a simple function of research. Think how often we are told that we ought to be doing more research to ensure a higher rate of innovation (or growth). This belief seems to be based on a simple model of the innovation process:

Research⟶ Development (invention) ⟶Investment⟶ New products / New processes

If innovation did flow easily from research we should find, given the relation between innovation and growth, a strong statistical relation between research and growth in product per head. The statistics on research are far from satisfactory, but the possible errors

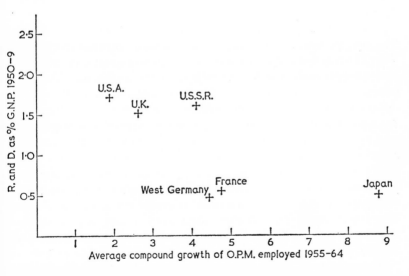

* From *Science and the City*, Hambros Bank and New Scientist, November 1963.

are not sufficient to upset the conclusion that there is not a close relationship between research and growth.

The chart above shows the relationship between the approximate expenditure on R and D expressed as a percentage of GNP and (with a five-year time lag) growth in output per man (OPM) employed.

R and D in advanced countries are necessary but far from sufficient conditions of rapid growth.

There is no need to labour this point in the City. If it believed that research was a *sufficient* condition of innovation and growth, it would not be concerned about the finance of innovation.

I. DEVELOPMENT GAP

A more sophisticated version of the research-innovation model runs in terms of a chain of relations and allows for weak links in the chain. There have been many suggestions that in the United Kingdom the development link is weak. There is in fact a tendency to shout 'weak link' when any of our 'science' is developed first by another country, though not to shout 'strong link' when the opposite happens. In fact, as Carter and I showed in *Industry and Technical Progress*, the weak link is often research.

A weak development link may be caused by (i) lack of balance in the supply and/or deployment of scientific manpower. (ii) an inappropriate industrial structure, (iii) a time-scale of final exploitation thought excessive by the firm or firms concerned. There is strong evidence for the belief that our manpower supply is un-balanced – 'too few engineers relative to scientists' – and that it is wrongly deployed – 'too many in research relative to development and production'. It is also clear that in many industries firms are too small to finance and organize the optimum development effort. This problem of industrial structure has not been solved by government or co-operative research associations, which are better at research than development; nor by Government development contracts, which flow more easily from defence needs and in any case are often inefficient because the industrial structure is, or was, wrong – the aircraft industry provides an excellent example here.

However, even if structure is appropriate, the development link may be weak because the choice criteria are wrong. Expenditure on development is (apart from the scientific fun involved)* only worth-while if (i) a technical solution is likely and (ii) the solution would be commercially valuable. Failure to consider both (i) and (ii) has led to a great deal of inefficiency in the United Kingdom development process. The economics of R and D is a much neglected problem in United Kingdom industry, and the cost of neglect – the growth foregone – is high.[1]

Some developments may take a decade or two to reach full commercial exploitation. Private firms may not be prepared to put money into developments of this kind even though they may be in the social interest. This is partly a problem of structure, partly of the supply of risk capital.

2. RISK CAPITAL

The investment link in the chain may also be weak. Sometimes innovation presents no problem of finance. The R and D process may make possible a new process formula which reduces loss or increases quality. A new process might also be embodied in normal replace-ment. But often new finance is required, and in so far as it is difficult to raise finance because the firm is new, or in so far as company directors have a very strong aversion to risk, the investment in innovation will not take place or take place late, perhaps when other countries have established the new method. Many scientists have alleged that one important reason why we are often slow into new fields is that the crucial investment decisions are made by bankers and accountants who have a strong aversion to risk and are unable to comprehend the impact of the scientific revolution.

In an important sense development reduces the risk of investment in innovation. By building pilot plants and prototypes and conducting detailed design studies, it becomes possible to get a much better idea of the scale of investment that would be involved, the costs of production, and the quality of performance of the potential new product. From this new information calculations of the potential yield from investment in the project change from guesses to 'guesstimates'.

Even so the forecasts and results of investment in innovation

* It is worth stressing, because of the capacity of interested parties to overlook the obvious, that for a given R and D expenditure, the greater the growth-effect the smaller R and D as a percentage of GNP. It is odd that so many scientists should advocate a high R and D percentage, not on grounds of scientific fun, but on grounds of economic growth.

seldom tally. In the study which Carter and I made, five or six years ago, the correlation between forecast and achieved yields on investment in innovation was only 0·13. In general over-estimation and under-estimation proved equally likely, which meant that firms with many investment projects tended to come out right on average.[2]

Although development is meant to reduce the number of unknowns, the outcome of investment in innovation is often unpredictable. It follows that the outcome of investment in development is even more unpredictable. Investment of resources in development is thus more speculative than investment in innovation, though for any given project the amount at risk in the latter will often, though not always, be much greater. I stress this because the problem of risk capital is often assumed to be a problem of putting an invention into production, whereas the more critical problem may be the finance to make the invention possible. This is fairly obvious when we think of the risk capital required for the *development* of atomic power stations and supersonic airliners; it is less obvious but no less important in the many less dramatic cases that come up, or should come up, within very many firms. A shortage of risk capital in this more general sense may help to explain our high ratio of research expenditure to development expenditure.

3. REACTION TO RISK

In considering the resources made available for investment in both development and innovation we need to look at (i) the attitude to risk and (ii) the attitude to potential earnings at different points of time.

If we ignore the 'time profile' of potential earnings, we can simplify the development problem by putting a commercial value to the planned invention and introducing probability estimates to calculate a probable yield. (The same procedure can be used to estimate probable yield from investment in innovation.) The following examples show what is involved.

	Project a	Project b
1. Commercial value of planned invention (£)	100,000	400,000
2. Planned development outlay (£)	70,000	70,000
3. Probability of invention resulting from this outlay	0·8	0·4
4. Probable value (1 × 3) (£)	80,000	160,000
5. Probable yield $\left(\dfrac{4-2}{2}\right) \times 100$	14%	130%

On this form of figuring, *Project b* is much more attractive. Many firms and outside investors, however, would not touch it, regarding a project with a probability of success of only 0·4 as 'too much of a gamble'. Yet if, of ten *a*-type projects, eight went according to plan and two were 'dead losses' the yield would be only $12\frac{1}{2}\%$, whereas if four of ten *b*-type projects went according to plan and six failed completely the overall yield would be more than 50%.

If *a*-type projects are accepted and *b*-type rejected, whether due to a search for near certainty on each project or an inability to 'average', the yield on investment in innovation will be kept needlessly low.

If, furthermore, *a*-type projects are dominantly improvements on existing processes and products while the *b*-type projects entail radical changes in, and the creation of, new technologies, then even a large expenditure on Rand D (especially if a large part is defence Rand D) would not put a country in the forefront of innovation. That the United Kingdom despite its large Rand D percentage, has imported a high proportion of important innovations[3] may seem to suggest that the approach to investment in development and innovation has been too cautious. This is certainly one possible explanation. Clear evidence on this, particularly at the development stage, is lacking. On investment in innovation there is no evidence that United Kingdom businessmen and financiers set higher standards of yield than do the Americans and Germans. What I am inclined to stress more is the development projects that are not considered. Here it is not possible to make a clear distinction between the efforts of a shortage of risk capital in the general sense I have given it, and the 'development gap'.

4. WAITING FOR YIELDS

So far I have ignored the problem of time. Some projects give quick yields; others (and particularly so if they have started at the research stage) take a long time to pay off. Given the cost of capital, some form of discounting is required to make possible rational choice between projects with different earnings profiles and to judge whether a project with a very long payback period is worthwhile.

But what discount rate should be used? The present value of a project equals:

$$\frac{P_1}{(1+d)} + \frac{P_2}{(1+d)^2} + \ldots + \frac{P_n}{(1+d)^n} - C$$

where C is the present value of the initial capital outlay, d the discount rate reflecting the cost of capital to the firm, and $P_1 \ldots P_n$ the cash proceeds in periods $1 \ldots n$. Clearly, the greater the discount rate the smaller the significance of future earnings. If the rate of discount is 10%, in five years time a cash flow of £175, and in ten years time £289, will be needed to match one of £100 now. Firms that use the payback criterion and set a short period are in effect using a *very* high discount rate and so eliminating automatically projects which mature slowly. The use of high discount rates must eliminate many worth-while potential innovations. The use of the internal rate of return formula

$$C = \frac{P_1}{(1 + r)} + \frac{P_2}{(1 + r)^2} + \cdots + \frac{P_n}{(1 + r)^n}$$

where r is the internal rate of return, instead of the present value formula, when d is the cost of capital to the firm, can also have the same effect.* Yet often these projects with a relatively long gestation period will have the greatest innovation content and growth potential.

The use of the short payback criterion appears to be less common here than in the United States, but this does not mean that R and D yields may not have been depressed by short-time horizons. For the appropriate time horizon in any firm is partly a function of size and, given the greater average size of United States firms and the greater willingness of their Government to assist with civil R and D contracts, their time horizons may have been longer in crucial cases. This is a very important problem in the economics of R and D on which we need much more research. There is, of course, an important implication. Given our size and our shortages in scientific manpower, if we are to extend time horizons in certain directions our R and D effort will have to be more selective if R and D yields are to rise. The element of judgement or hunch will always be important, and to have possible alternative sources of finance for big projects will be a great advantage.

5. RESEARCH AND GROWTH

There are other reasons for the absence of statistical relationship between research and growth which should be mentioned.

(*a*) *Defence.* In both the United Kingdom and the United States a high proportion of R and D is for defence. The 'growth fallout' has been relatively small.

---

* These two formulae will give the same result only 'at the margin' – when the internal rate of return is equal to the cost of raising capital.

(*b*) *Purchase of knowhow.* There is a considerable international trade in technical knowledge. There is no known optimum relationship between 'own Rand D' and purchase of knowhow. It is certainly possible to substitute one for the other; it will certainly be cheaper at times to innovate via the purchase of knowhow. So long as some other countries go in for Rand D it may even pay a country to rely on the purchase of know-how.

In 1960, France received N.F. 108 million and paid N.F. 273 million for technological knowhow. The 'adverse balance' is thought to be even greater in the cases of Germany and Japan. By contrast the United States receives six times as much in fees and royalties as it pays out. The high Rand D in the United States may well induce more growth abroad than at home. The high growth rates but low Rand D rates in Germany, Japan, France, and Australia are due in some measure to economies in own Rand D made possible by purchase of foreign knowhow. There is good reason to doubt whether the United Kingdom should be trying to rely so much on own Rand D in many fields.

(*c*) There is, however, more to growth through science than investment in innovation. However brilliant the technical innovation, however well timed the investment, if it is not managed well the growth potential will be squandered. There is no doubt that this has been a factor of significance in the United Kingdom.

(*d*) But even if we overcame impediments to the use of science it would be wrong to expect equal Rand D percentages to produce equal growth rates in different countries. In some countries innovation will have uncomplicated growth effects. In other countries (and I think the United Kingdom is in this class) a great deal of innovation will be required to avoid decline consequent on changes in other countries. Mature industrial countries will at times be somewhat in the position of Alice in the Garden of Flowers, where it took all the running to stay in the same place and faster than that to get anywhere. Fortunately, going 'faster than that' can get us off this garden path.

REFERENCES

1. C. F. CARTER and B. R. WILLIAMS, *Science in Industry* (Oxford University Press, 1959).
2. *Idem, Investment in Innovation*, Chapter 7 (Oxford University Press, 1958).
3. D. BURN, *Progress*, September 1962.

V

Technical Innovation:
the Key to Faster Growth?*

The United Kingdom's growth record is rather like its weather – bad enough to cause strong complaints, but not bad enough to induce drastic action. In the past three-quarters of a century, average annual growth rates in real product a man-year in the United Kingdom and the Common Market countries were between 1 and 1·5%, with the United Kingdom, Holland, and Italy towards the bottom of the range, and France and Germany at the top. In this same period the United States and Sweden had growth rates of 2% and Japan of almost 3%.

In the post-war years the United Kingdom's growth rate has been above its long-term average (rather more so than in the United States). But in the Common Market countries (other than Belgium) and in Japan growth rates have been very much above their long-term average. Between 1950 and 1960 the growth rate was just over 1·5% in the United Kingdom. Yet it was about 3·5% in Holland and France, 4·5% in West Germany and in Italy and 6% in Japan. In the last five years the United Kingdom's growth rate has fallen further behind the Japanese, but come closer to those in the Common Market countries. Unfortunately, this has been caused by a fall of the rate in Western Europe, not by a rise in the United Kingdom.

Why has the United Kingdom growth rate fallen behind that even in comparable West-European countries? Is it simply that our investment rate is low? By comparison with the Common Market countries the United Kingdom's investment rate has been low. In the 1950's gross fixed investment in the United Kingdom was only 14·5% of GNP compared with 17% in France and between 20% and 22% in Italy, West Germany, and Holland. Belgium's investment rate was only 15·5% but then its growth rate was nearly down to the United Kingdom level.

It would be wrong, however, to conclude from this evidence that

* From *The Times Review of Industry*, December 1962.

the problem of growth is simply a problem of investment rates. Between 1950 and 1960 there were some remarkable national differences in the relations between growth and investment. In West Germany, the incremental capital-output ratio was 3; that is to say the investment rate (gross investment as a percentage of GNP) was three times the growth rate of GNP. In Italy the ratio was $3\frac{1}{2}$, in France $4\frac{1}{2}$, in Holland just under $5\frac{1}{2}$, and in Belgium just over $5\frac{1}{2}$. In the United Kingdom the ratio was 6.

I. INVESTMENT AND OUTPUT

It might appear that high investment rates and low incremental capital-output ratios were closely related. This, however, was not so. Holland had an investment rate higher than both the German and French rates, but an incremental capital-output ratio higher even than the French; France had an investment rate little higher than Belgium's, but a much lower incremental capital-output ratio.

But even if there were a marked tendency for high investment rates and low incremental capital-output ratios to appear together, and vice versa, it would not be safe to conclude that high incremental capital-output ratios could be overcome by pushing up the investment rate. Obviously, there might be a tendency for investment rates to be high because of the high productivity of new investment, and vice versa. Where a low investment rate was caused by the low productivity of new investment, a Government decision to force up the investment rate without making other changes would soon be checked by balance of payments difficulties.

In the United Kingdom, there has been a persistent tendency for growth to create balance of payments problems. Governments have reacted to this with financial restrictions to protect the pound, so helping to create erratic annual movements in production. Annual rates of growth in industrial production have been:

1954–55	1955–56	1956–57	1957–58	1958–59	1959–60	1960–61	1961–62
6	0	2	−2	5	7	1	$2\frac{1}{2}$

Fluctuations in the demand for United Kingdom exports explain part of this movement, but 'stop-go' financial measures have certainly exaggerated the fluctuations. Some writers go so far as to blame these financial measures for the relatively poor average performance of the United Kingdom economy.

In fact, few of the main problems of the United Kingdom economy can be traced to the Government's 'stop-go' financial policy. The causal link is the other way round. It is the persistent tendency of expansion to create balance of payments problems that explains the successive financial restrictions. The form and timing of restriction has often been wrong, but this has probably been more important in creating fluctuations in annual rates of growth than in reducing the average rate or growth. The most important questions are why United Kingdom economic expansion has led so quickly to balance of payments problems; why in the highly favourable overall financial conditions since the war investment in innovation has been so weak; why capital expenditure has been so dependent on growth in the home demand for durable consumer goods.

Professor Kindleberger has suggested recently that growth based upon capital formation presents more difficulties for the balance of payments than growth proceeding from technical change. This suggested dichotomy between capital formation and technical change may appear strange. Surely, it may be said, technical change in industry requires capital formation? The answer is that some technical change does require capital formation, but by no means all; some increases in output a man are explained by increased capital inputs, but certainly not all of them.

Recently the Norwegian statistician Odd Aukrust, puzzling about why the high post-war rates of investment in Norway and Sweden had not led to high rates of growth, came to the conclusion that 'the human factor (organization, professional skills, and technical knowledge) is at least as important to the rate of economic growth as the volume of physical capital'. For Norway 1948–55 he calculated that of the growth rate of 3·39% a year, 0·46% came from increased labour, 1·12% from increased capital, and 1·81% from better organization. He concluded that the possibilities of accelerating economic growth by increased investments have been overrated, but that economic growth could probably be 'considerably increased if we make new efforts in the fields of education and scientific research'.

2. CAIRNCROSS'S CONCLUSION

In the United Kingdom, Professor Cairncross reached a similar conclusion by a rather different route. From rough but reasonable assumptions about the productivity and composition of investment, he calculated that only one-third of the increase in output was attributable to investment. He concluded that it is indifference to the possibilities of technical progress far more than lack of capital that prevents a more rapid improvement in productivity and income. In the United States, the statistical studies of Fabricant and Kendrick point to the conclusion that at least three-quarters of the increase in output a man-hour since 1900 is attributable to technical progress rather than to the formation of capital.

It is obvious that the United Kingdom cannot expect mere investment to solve its growth problems. Technical progress is a vital condition of growth. But before we draw any policy conclusions we had better be clear about the nature of this technical progress. As used by Aukrust, Cairncross, and Kendrick it is a catch-ball. It covers all increases in output not the result of mere increases in quantities of labour and capital. Technical progress, thus, includes the effects of better organization, more effective labour (whether caused by better training or by a greater intensity of effort), improved materials (whether from discovery of new sources or from closer control following scientific research), besides the invention of new machines and processes to produce both old and new products.

Obviously some of this technical progress does not require any capital expenditure in industry. There is tremendous scope for growth through better industrial housekeeping. With the proper use of planning and control techniques it is usually possible to squeeze a greater output, and often a very much greater output, from existing equipment. The planning of design in relation to market potential, the planning of the supply and movement of materials and components, the planning of the use of plant and labour to ensure the lowest cost completion of production targets, create the conditions of low capital-output ratios. To achieve these plans, controls are needed – stock control, production control, quality control, and budgetary control. Because the lack of efficient planning and control is one of the outstanding features of the United Kingdom industry, attention to them could bring greater growth from existing plants.

With given plant, the additional yields from better industrial housekeeping will fall off in time, but whenever new plant is installed there is almost certain to be a chance to push output well above the capacity for which it was designed. There are many known instances where good planning and control has gradually forced the achieved rate of output to more than twice that of the designed capacity.

Research contributes a great deal of this form of growth. A better knowledge of the nature of materials and processes and of the way to maintain control over operating conditions makes possible reductions in spoiled or defective work or increases in the speed of throughput. Research may also lead to the design of higher quality products and so to an increased value of output from given plants.

Many new methods and most new products require investment in new plant. When talking of new ways of producing old goods, it is usual to distinguish between capital-saving, labour-saving, and neutral innovations. In a capital-saving innovation there are economies in the capital required a unit output at designed capacity. Thus in recent designs for nuclear power stations, the capital cost a unit output has been almost halved. In a labour-saving innovation there are labour economies a unit output at designed capacity. In oil refining, the change from the Houdry method to fluid catalylic cracking more than halved the labour input a unit output. In a neutral innovation there are economies in both labour and capital. There are several examples of automation in which economy in labour and (because of almost continuous machine operation) economy in capital a unit output, almost balance.

3. ECONOMY IN CAPITAL

Where the process innovation achieves economy in capital a unit output there will be a downward pressure on the incremental capital-output ratio. But whatever the type of process innovation, if it is profitable it will stimulate investment and growth. Even if innovations are neutral or labour saving they will in fact help to reduce the incremental capital-output ratio if their capital a unit output is relatively low. Thus, if, because of labour-saving or neutral innovations, investment in the electronics industry grew relative to investment in agriculture or hydroelectric power the probable effect would be a fall in the incremental capital output ratio for the community. We can say the same of innovation leading to a new industry if its capital a unit output is relatively low.

Because in its design an innovation is capital saving, it does not follow that it will be so in practice. If because of misjudgement of growth in the market, or of rivals' capacity, the new plant is operated far below capacity, it may not be capital saving a unit output. Labour-saving or neutral innovations may, as we have seen, raise the community's growth rate relative to its investment rate, but clearly this is much less likely where the investment in them is excessive.

Whether it is in capital-saving, labour-saving, or neutral innovations, investment sufficient to create excess capacity must make the investment rate excessive for the achieved growth of output. In recent years this has been so in coal, chemicals, electrical engineering, steel, and vehicles. A similar effect was created in the electricity industry by installing nuclear power stations at a time when by contrast with conventional stations they were extravagant in capital.

Fast growth depends on the appropriate balance between opportunities for technical progress (in the various forms considered) and pressure to use them. Opportunities come from increasing scientific and technical knowledge making possible new physical processes and products, and from increasing understanding of human organization, making possible more efficient planning and control. These opportunities may be imported from abroad, they may come from the United Kingdom's own organized R and D, or they may come from individual inventors and improvers.

In modern industries, both R and D and the use of new methods (from whatever source) require the employment of highly qualified manpower. By comparison with competitor countries our manpower position is not entirely satisfactory. In 1958 the United Kingdom had 16·8% of its 15–19 age-group in full-time education. West Germany with 17·6% was a little ahead of the United Kingdom. France with 30·8% was far ahead of us. In the 20–24 age-group we had only 2·4% in full-time education, compared with 3·8% in France and 4·6% in West Germany. In 1959 in the United Kingdom, there was a recognized shortage of qualified scientists and engineers equal to 10% of supply.

In R and D the United Kingdom's overall expenditure compares more than favourably with that in France and Germany. But the United Kingdom R and D effort is dominated by defence and, although overall expenditure is high, there are many signs of inadequacy in civil fields – in mechanical and civil engineering, machine tools, metals, and so on. The relative importance of the United Kingdom's contribution to post-war process and product innovations is perhaps less than might be reasonably expected from the magnitude of total R and D effort.

4. MORE CIVIL RESEARCH

It would be foolish for any country to aim at self-sufficiency in invention. But given the cost of getting innovations on licence and the profit to be derived for getting in on a good thing early, the United Kingdom should certainly aim to develop more profitable new processes and products itself. In the United Kingdom there is a good argument for more *civil* research and (much more) development in promising fields. This places a big responsibility on the Government to identify the most promising fields, to push up R and D where the industry (whether for reasons of stupidity or structure) is not making a big enough effort. Since research now cannot have a big impact for some time, it is important to think of today's promising research projects in terms of economic trends in four or five year's time. The Government's strategy on civil research has been poor because it has refrained from this difficult form of intellectual activity.

More could usefully be done to increase opportunities for innovation. What of the pressures on British businessmen both to create and use them? For a long time now the pressures have been weak. In the private sector the potential pressures have been kept weak by high import duties, by the under-valuation of sterling and by a network of restrictive practices. The Restrictive Practices Act has helped to increase pressures in some sectors of the economy, but while tariffs remain high the pressures to innovate and modernize will be relatively weak. In the public sector, Governments have done little to provide a substitute for market pressures and penalties. Indeed, at times Governments have done just the opposite. Because of this it has been possible for nationalized industries to engage in openly uneconomic investment projects and to be extremely dilatory in the search for innovations and adoption of established processes.

I have said nothing of the burdens of tax and little of monetary and fiscal policy. This is because I think these have been of secondary importance in the post-war boom years. If Government policy had been more successful in creating bigger opportunities and pressures for technical progress, investment would not have seemed so sensitive to financial restrictions. Indeed, at times, to ensure reasonable stability, we would probably have needed stronger measures of financial control!

VI

Some Conditions
of Useful Competition*

The Restrictive Trade Practices Act of 1956 marks a significant change of view about the social benefits of competition. Even in the 1948 Act setting up the Monopolies Commission the question whether restrictive practices were contrary to the public interest was left wide open. But not so now. There are (at least) two explanations of this change in attitude: (i) that the long period of full employment has changed the relevant problems and shifted attention from excess capacity to short supply and restrictions on trade; and (ii) that a reaction against Civil Service control of industry has carried with it a reaction against Trade Association control of trade.

Times do change, and it is doubtless appropriate that attitudes to competition should on certain occasions change with them. Unfortunately the change of opinion often seems less soundly based: when there is excess capacity and cut-throat competition we seemingly become very conscious of the virtues of price stability and blow up the limitations of competition into a more general theory 'in praise of monopoly'; and when times are good and supplies are short, we tend to focus on the evils of restriction and exalt 'the virtues of competition'. If in the near future we have more take-overs and consolidations, the view that restrictive practices protect us from further monopolization may well become fashionable.

This tendency for fashion is a sign that our theory of competition is incomplete. The economic analysis of competition, such as it is, may be broken into two parts. The first concerns the effect of competition on the *relation* between prices and costs; the second concerns the *level* of costs. The first has been the main preoccupation of economists, though the second is more likely to be important to our material standards of living. The reason for this emphasis on the less important problem is that it is adapted to the economist's usual techniques of

* Paper read at the York meeting of the British Association for the Advancement of Science, 1959.

analysis. By contrast, explanation of the level of costs involves questions of technology and sociology. Nonetheless in dealing with the effects of competition we must take such things into account. My concern in this paper is not to produce a complete theory of competition but to pick out certain dynamic factors which may have an important bearing on the power of competition to induce product and process innovation.

1. COMPETITION AND ALLOCATION

Competition, on the usual static assumptions, leads to the elimination of surplus profit. If competition is perfect, price will move to equality with average and marginal cost in marginal firms (or in all firms if economic rents are capitalized). This gives what is often called an optimum allocation of resources.

If there are few firms, or if there are special markets due to quality (or pseudo-quality) differences, competition may still eliminate profits, though price would not also equal marginal cost, and there would be 'unused economies of scale'.

If there are few firms and also barriers to entry and/or a restrictive group-control of prices and distribution, surplus profits may exist. In this case 'economies of scale' may not exist though price would be greater than marginal cost. To sweep away restrictive practices might increase production and eliminate profit. In so doing it would create 'unused economies of scale', unless competition was made perfect—an unlikely event in most trades.

Unfortunately this type of curve shifting, useful though it may be in lectures, tells us very little about the virtues of competition. Suppose that there are 'unused economies of scale' due to non-homogeneous production which is not dependent on restrictive practices. What would be the cost of eliminating non-homogeneity relative to the gains of using economies of scale? The theory cannot tell us. For this and other reasons the perfect-competition case is frequently a useless norm. There is a rather important procedural point that sometimes obscures this. It is quite usual in static theory to assume not simply that production functions are given but, that in the existing state of science and technology the techniques of production of every firm are perfect: in Stigler's words 'economists are interested only in the best techniques'. It follows that any firm making say a TV set is assumed to make as good a TV set as is possible in the given conditions of technology and factor costs. Brands are then objectively irrelevant: they only describe qualities achieved at higher cost. By implication, branding goods is simply a device to build up irrational consumer preferences.

2. INNOVATION AND MARKET IMPERFECTIONS

There are, of course, many attempts to build up irrational consumer preferences through advertising, where the principle of excellence by association is worked very hard indeed. But 'product differentiation' has a far greater importance than this: it is often an inevitable by-product of innovation. Some innovations are process innovations that leave the product unaffected, as for example design improvements in atomic power stations. But often innovations change products, or create new ones. Because they do not occur simultaneously in all relevant firms innovations create market imperfections such as product differences and single sellers. To get this in perspective we need perhaps to think rather less of detergents, cosmetics, and cereals, and rather more of electronics, airplanes, rockets, machine tools, drugs, and man-made fibres.

In considering product differentiation the nature of the buyer should also be considered. The householder when faced with a great variety of cars, refrigerators, detergents, drip-dry fabrics, and the like may find it difficult to judge their precise qualities, even with the stout aid of *Which?* and *Shopper's Guide*. But firms are better placed, and firms in fact buy more goods. In 1954 households bought goods and services worth £11,500 million, whereas the sum of intermediate output sold to firms, capital formation (other than private houses) and exports, was £16,000 million.

In the course of time the 'technical knowhow' in an innovation will spread. Unless patent protection is both unusually good and used restrictively the 'market imperfections' will diminish as knowledge of the new processes is acquired by other firms. In time, then, 'the best techniques' will be spread more widely. But as one set of market imperfections is reduced later innovations will create others.

The unreality of the textbook assumption that only the best techniques are used is not, however, solely due to this time factor. There are also differences in technical knowhow apart from those incidental to current innovation. One of the outstanding features of some many-firm industries without strong restrictive practices is the

F

big gap between the most and the least efficient. This brings me to the dynamic section of the theory of competition—namely, the effect of competition on the level of costs. Does competition eliminate the high cost producers? If so, how? Does competition induce innovation, and, if so, in what manner?

3. ELIMINATING THE UNFIT

It is usual to suppose that any excess-profits earned by the most efficient firms will attract investment in new capacity. This will lower prices and bankrupt the inefficient firms. This investment in new capacity may come from new firms or from the most efficient firms. It is from new firms we suppose that they acquire the technical knowledge and competence that the marginal firms failed to acquire. If the marginal firms are run by incompetents this is a reasonable supposition, though just how common is plain incompetence in contrast to relative (and temporary) incompetence is unknown. Expansion by the intra-marginal firms, using their surplus profits, is often more likely. In so far as this is the process, the elimination of inefficiency will reduce the number of competitors.

There has been very little study of how far, or fast, this process is likely to go. In certain multi-firm industries that I have studied the process did not go very far or very fast so long as there were no major changes in technology, or in the degree of competition from substitutes. The more efficient firms were inclined to expand with the total market and not ahead of it. Once, however, there were major changes in technology and in competition from substitutes the more efficient firms did expand ahead of the market.[1] In this process I found no significant difference between industries that used restrictive practices such as common pricing and those that did not. The thing that mattered was the opportunity to innovate, and the uneven distribution of capacity to use that opportunity.

The 'plain incompetents' are supposed to go bankrupt. By contrast the 'relative or temporary incompetents' are supposed to nearn Because of them and of enterprising outsiders capacity will increase and prices and profits will fall. In a system of free competition the only way to restore profits is to cut process costs or introduce an effective new product. Thus in so far as the competition does eliminate profit it is presumed to induce firms to innovate to restore profits.

4. THE CHANCE TO INNOVATE

We need then to ask whether innovation is easy? Is it easy to finance? Is it easy to manage?

Sometimes innovation is easy. To a manufacturer who has been pestered to produce to closer specifications the appearance of a new machine tool or an automatic control that fits readily into the existing processes may be a 'god-send'. In some cases industrial research is concerned with finding answers to problems posed by the production or sales staff, and the difficulty may be in the research itself and not in the application of the results. In many cases, however, firms find the application of industrial research more difficult than the research itself. Using the results of the research may involve a radical change in process—in the type of machinery used or in the human division of labour, or in both; it may also involve the introduction of new commodities with largely unknown market potentials.[2]

In the same way and for much the same reasons both the finance and the management of innovation may or may not be a problem. The finance of transfer machines in the motor car industry after the war was no great problem, nor even the finance of tunnel ovens in the multi-firm pottery industry;[3] in both cases the innovations helped to ease critical shortages. The finance of one of our great post-war innovations – atomic power stations – has not been an acute problem, though without the initial and continuing Government expenditure on R and D it would have been. The finance of the proposed very-high-speed passenger aircraft is a problem – both the potential financial yield and the time it would take to get a yield are great unknowns.

Ease of finance may or may not be connected with size. Some small firms with a fine record in managing innovation have shown very high growth rates. Thus one firm in the electronics industry from a start ten years ago with a few hundred pounds, two working directors and three employees now has total assets of almost £1¾ million. Other small firms in slower-growth industries have had more difficulty in financing innovation. The raising of 'new money' by a company new to the Stock Exchange is expensive and difficult, and in any case the new issue market is not suitable for issues smaller than £50,000 or for companies with assets less than £100,000. There are many other sources of finance but knowledge of these sources and the ability to exploit them is very unevenly spread – a matter which may be as important to the spread of new technologies as the uneven distribution of technical knowledge.

Obviously some types of innovation are inappropriate to small firms, as for example a large investment in an innovation that is either very risky or probably has an extended pay-off period. But choosing the right type and amount of innovation is an important management problem to large as well as to small firms.[4] One aspect of this problem is choosing the right level of investment in invention.

One of the most important recent changes in industry has been the growth of this form of investment. In the United States (for which there are usable statistics) industrial RandD grew from 0·04% of national income in 1920 to 0·1% in 1930, to 0·8% in 1950. There has also been a growth in other research the results of which are used for industrial research and together they constitute 1½% of national income. In the United Kingdom the percentage is perhaps a little higher.

A large part of this industrial RandD is concentrated in larger firms. In the United States half the industrial scientists and engineers are employed in eighty of the biggest firms; in the United Kingdom more than half of those employed on RandD were in sixty-one *establishments*. In one of his later works, *Capitalism, Socialism and Democracy*, Schumpeter considered this form of growth and concluded (p. 106) that, given the cost of innovation, the growth of RandD as a management technique has made the large-scale establishment or unit of control the most powerful engine of economic progress and that perfect competition has become not only impossible but also inferior as an instrument of progress.

In this field it is unwise to generalize too comprehensively about the impact of industrial research on size. Sometimes large-scale organization is required, e.g. atomic energy. But RandD is not restricted to large firms; still less is innovation. Indeed, radical changes in processes and products still very often come from small firms and from people outside the recognized trade. It is also important to stress that innovation is not always directly dependent on RandD in the industry concerned. Think of the impact of automatic controls and computers on a wide variety of firms in other industries. Innovation then does not always require that the innovating firms have a research department, though it generally does require the employment of scientists or engineers in production departments. Furthermore, innovations in one industry frequently require co-operation from suppliers of materials or machines. Some of these suppliers may be small specialist firms that concentrate on particular developments. This is most obvious in electronics.

Opportunities to innovate and the mode of innovating vary, particularly between science-based and craft-based industries. The science-based industries are in fact based on university research in Chemistry and Physics, and require the services of scientists and technologists. These are provided as part of the normal process of higher education; whereas the science underlying the craft-based industries is not. In those industries where technology is based on art rather than science less attention is given to R and D, which is much less productive for a given expenditure on it than in science-based industries. Where research that *might* shift the technology from art to science is very expensive and long term, it is not likely to be generated by the competitive process. Hence the need for research, probably Government sponsored, on a co-operative basis. Often differences in progressiveness between industries are imputed to size rather than to this difference in the technological basis of production. Galbraith, for example, makes this mistake.

5. THE PRESSURE TO INNOVATE

Given a good supply of scientists and technologists and a sufficient background of relevant scientific information, firms can create profitable R and D departments to develop new products and new processes. Under these conditions the impact of falling profit on innovation will be much more direct and certain. The pressure to innovate will, however, exist apart from a fall in profit. The process of R and D increases the possibility of substitute methods and products. Firms know that their profits may be undermined at any time by radical developments in other firms or in other industries. Yet in science-based firms at least, this fear encourages rather than inhibits action precisely because research can create innovations. (In craft-based firms the expectation of technical progress often has the opposite effect.) Furthermore, research is just one of a group of related management techniques. Any firm that appoints a R and D department, a work-study section, technical sales staff and so on, creates groups of people with an interest in pushing innovations. There will in fact be strong internal pressures to innovate.

It follows from all this that any tendencies associated with R and D to reduce the number of firms or to increase (temporarily at least) the non-homogeneity of production is unlikely to reduce the pressure of competition. Competition between the few in innovating industries is likely to be more intense and effective than competition between the many in technically stagnant industries. Mere numbers cannot ensure useful competition.

6. POSITIVE CONDITIONS OF COMPETITION

There are many industries in the United Kingdom economy that spend little on development and employ few scientists and technologists. In these industries (as Carter and I showed in some detail in *Industry and Technical Progress*) the capacity even to use the innovations of others is small. This in turn affects the capacity of those others to innovate. What innovations a firm can make or is pressed to make must depend on the help or stimulus it gets from its customers, suppliers, and competitors. There is in fact a *chain of relations* between firms that plays a dominating part in the speed or slowness with which firms in any country apply science to industry. The nature of this chain of relations, which affects both the degree and effectiveness of competition, is very much affected by the overall supply of scientists, technologists and technicians; that is to say very much affected by *human* capital in which the Americans, for example, make a larger investment than we do. To explain the greater competitive pressure in the United States economy I would look to this much more than to Anti-Trust.

The point that I wish to stress is that the creation of the opportunity to innovate is a most important condition of useful competition. Yet this opportunity is not created by competition. It requires a system of education and provision for a great deal of fundamental scientific activity. This helps to explain a puzzling thing about competition, namely its apparent opposition to the principle of co-operation on which science and law and, indeed, business organization itself are based. Competition in fact works within a framework not provided by itself.

What is the bearing of all this on legislation about monopoly and restrictive practices?

If an industry is science-based does even monopoly matter? It does, I think, for two reasons.

(*a*) In industrial R and D there are thousands of research projects that might be chosen. The problem is to choose those most likely to lead to innovation. Without competitive pressure it would be easy for scientists to forget that they were supposed to be doing industrial research, and, in so far as this happened, monopoly could increase the development gap between invention and innovation.

(*b*) There are many examples of innovations which were made by outsiders and about which the experts in the trade, confined by an accepted framework of thought, were very sceptical. The chance for the 'outsider' or for a new man with experience in other industries to get his ideas applied may be better when the industry is not a monopoly.

The chance for the unorthodox is also greater if it is relatively easy to start new firms. Unorthodox ideas are often not easy to finance. Even if a firm gets started on a small scale the high level of tax makes it difficult to expand. New methods to finance the growth of firms with fresh technological ideas would help to create the conditions of more effective competition. Three things might help. Tax concessions for new firms would help, though it would be difficult to prevent abuses. State grants for development might help more, with the National Research Development Corporation perhaps as a suitable body to administer development grants. The institution of more firms to do R and D on contract would help even more. This, which the United Kingdom economy requires anyway, could be used by new and small firms to improve their growth prospects. It would make a big difference to the United Kingdom economy if the research associations developed an aggressive approach to development and really sold the idea of sponsored R and D.

What of restrictive practices such as common pricing? What is their likely effect on competition in innovation?

Common pricing, it is often said, is a way of preserving inefficient firms, a way which, if there is excess capacity, requires quotas for its maintenance. If it is simply a way of preserving the inefficient there is little to be said for it. Common pricing, however, *need* not protect the inefficient, and in certain circumstances may encourage efficiency. Suppose that due to a depression or a new technique there is excess capacity in the industry. Cut-throat competition may develop. This may not eliminate the excess capacity quickly and while it lasts the low level of profit and the uncertainty about the future may discourage much thought about further changes in technology. Common pricing and agreed terms or conditions of sale may help to provide a sufficient measure of stability to encourage long views which much innovation requires. The major difficulties are to get a form of common pricing that does not preserve the outmoded equipment, and to restore the opportunity for price competition when the excess capacity goes. It may be that common pricing has a temporarily useful role so long as an independent authority decides the basis of the pricing. Certainly a system of common pricing more fashioned to stimulate efficiency was adopted in the cement industry after the fforde Committee enquiry.

Another case I have in mind is where common pricing is associated with the development of a community of interest in new techniques. Then, so long as it is based on an average of costs heavily weighted by costs in the most efficient firms, common pricing may facilitate innovation. The Monopolies Commission thought that the Metal Windows Association Scheme was such an example. Tiles, I think, was another. Once, however, a community of interest in technical education and research is developed, this link between common pricing and technical progress is likely to weaken. But by then the likelihood that common pricing would be permitted to stop the expansion of innovations would be weakened. However, to ensure that, it is necessary to insist that common pricing should not be associated with effective control over distributive outlets except for very short periods. Here again, I think the main point to stress is the need to keep the way clear for the really big changes that may come later.

In a way these problems are similar to those thrown up by import duties. In certain trades at certain times protection may, by increasing and giving a sense of stability, induce innovation. Yet if provision is not made to review the duties from time to time the stimulating effect may be reversed. This is, I suspect, the case with restrictive practices. The difficulty is that they are generally decided and administered by just one of the interested parties, namely the Trade Association.

The conditions of effective competition cannot be laid down once and for all. Competition is a form of social control and like all social controls it cannot work autonomously. With change in such things as education, science, management competence and techniques, employment, international trade, and public finance, the conditions of effective competition change also.

REFERENCES

1. D. BURN (Editor), *The Structure of British Industry*, Chapters 8 and 17 (Cambridge University Press, 1958).

2. For predictive errors in innovation see C. F. CARTER and B. R. WILLIAMS, *Investment in Innovation*, Chapter 7 (Oxford University Press, 1958).

3. *Idem, Industry and Technical Progress*, Appendix III (Oxford University Press, 1957).

4. *Idem, Science in Industry*, Chapters 4–8 (Oxford University Press, 1959).

VII

Competitive Pressure and
Opportunity in Innovation*

There is no agreed theory of the relation between competition and efficiency. This may be explained by failure to consider fully the policy implications of static and dynamic methods of analysis, the ambiguity of the term efficiency, and the difficulty of defining degrees of competitive pressure in institutional terms.

Analysis in terms of 'efficiency' requires a clear statement of the desired result. When it is said approvingly that 'under perfect competition the consumer is king', the implied desired result is an allocation of resources to fit consumers' tastes as expressed in their expenditure patterns. The theory of optimum allocation of resources under given conditions of tastes, income distribution, and production functions, has been elaborated and refined *ad nauseam*. In the postulated conditions, there is no doubt that perfect competition is efficient. But the postulated conditions are very restrictive. The essence of economic progress, in which consumers have a strong interest, is a change in production functions. It follows that a static theory of optimum allocation is not a relevant theory unless it is just a simplification of the dynamic theory of optimum growth. In fact there has been little attempt to prove this, and several attempts to prove the contrary. Schumpeter has argued persuasively that the essential facts of the innovatory process 'are absent from the general scheme of economic life that yields the traditional propositions about perfect competition',[1] others have argued that there is a strong tension between individual choice and growth.[2]

The conditions of efficiency in allocating given resources to fit given tastes and incomes *may* be very different from the conditions of efficiency in producing some desired or desirable change in output per man-hour. One of the most significant modern developments is the growth of spending on industrial RandD to create opportunities to innovate. It is therefore important to discover

* Lecture given at the University of Melbourne, 1962.

whether, and in what way, competition stimulates such investment in innovation. This is a problem foreign to static theory, though in fact static theory has exercised a very strong influence on economists' approach to dynamic problems. Thus, examples of product differentiation are generally drawn from the market for consumers goods and stress brand differences in fields like cereals and cosmetics. When, however, we take examples such as aircraft engines, electronics, man-made fibres, and pharmaceuticals, we face the significant possibility that product differentiations may not be 'market imperfections' in the static sense, but an inevitable part of the process of man-made innovations required for the efficient pursuit of economic growth.

I. PRESSURE AND INNOVATION

The classical economists wrote much about the evils of monopoly, but very little about the virtues of competition. The explanation seems to be that they treated monopoly and competition as clear-cut and feasible alternatives. John Stuart Mill, for example, wrote that 'where competition is, monopoly is not; and monopoly in all its forms is the taxation of the industrious for the support of indolence if not of plunder'.

By contrast, Marx developed a pressure theory of innovation, of which the modern expression is to be found in Lange's essay 'On The Economic Theory of Socialism'. Competition among producers forces down prices and profits. In a multi-firm situation, pressure to restore profits takes the form of process or product innovations. Successful innovations re-create profits, but with the spread of the innovations supply is extended and prices and profits fall again. This creates a new pressure to innovate. To find an exposition of the growth through competition mechanism one goes not to Adam Smith but to Marx. In *The Communist Manifesto* Marx and Engels wrote that 'the bourgeoisie cannot live without constantly revolutionizing production' and they made it clear that this was the consequence of competitive pressure.

A recent variation on this pressure theory is to be found in Jack Downie's *The Competitive Process*. Downie treats the competitive process as a combination of the 'transfer mechanism' and the 'innovation mechanism'. The former – the growth of efficient at the expense of inefficient firms – is destructive of competition. But concentration is checked by the innovation mechanism: the inefficient firms faced with the threat of bankruptcy are pressed into innovatory activity; and, since innovation is treated as a function of pressure, they then increase their market share. Downie makes no generalization about the long-term relative strengths of these two mechanisms. By contrast, Marx did. This was because he assumed that the evolution of technology would give increasing economies of scale. Thus, 'big capital would eat little capital' and destroy competitive pressure. In other words, in Marx, even the innovation mechanism in the end operates to destroy competitive pressure, and with it role of the bourgeoisie as revolutionaries in production.

How far does this Marxian theory fit the facts? Given that Marx in some measure defines competition in terms of numbers – the cannibalistic habits of big capitalist brings the end of competition – we can test his theory by comparing the rate of innovation in multi-firm and few-firm industries. If this theory of competitive pressure is valid, the multi-firm industries should show high rates of innovation and vice versa. Yet many multi-firm industries without strong restrictive practices have shown low rates of innovation over quite long periods, though some few-firm industries have shown high rates of innovation. It follows that the Marxian theory of innovation is inadequate. Is it right to assume that technology *per se* is inherently dynamic? Are some technologies more inherently dynamic than others? If so, we have the problem that competitive pressure may be effective in some industries but not in others.

2. THE CONCENTRATION EFFECT

That the emphasis on research varies greatly between industries can be seen from Table 1, which shows that 1958 expenditure on R and D in the United Kingdom and the United States.

Large firms are dominant in industrial R and D. In both countries about 350 firms account for over 85% of spendings. In the United States each of these 350 firms employs more than 5,000 people; in the United Kingdom each of the 350 firms employs more than 2,000 people. Furthermore a very high proportion of large firms spend on R and D – over 80% in the 5,000 and over size group in the United States, and in the 2,000 and over size group in the United Kingdom. By contrast less than 20% of the smaller firms spend on R and D work.

In R and D work there are some important size effects. In sections of the chemical industry, a research team of less than twenty qualified scientists is unlikely to be worthwhile. In the United Kingdom such a team would cost more than £100,000 a year. In some industries (e.g. aircraft) the minimum cost is higher; in others (e.g. sections of the electronics industry) it is lower. Even though there is no evidence that there are continuing economies of scale in R and D activity, this 'threshold effect' is an important one.

The significance of industrial R and D and the special contribution of large firms has been generalized by Schumpeter and Galbraith. Schumpeter wrote that 'it is not sufficient to argue that because perfect competition is impossible under modern industrial conditions . . . the large-scale establishment or unit of control must be accepted as a necessary evil unseparable from the economic progress which it is prevented from sabotaging by the forces inherent in its productive apparatus. What we have got to accept is that it has come to be the most powerful engine of that progress. . . .'[3] Galbraith gave this doctrine a special North-American tone when he wrote that 'a benign Providence who, so far, has loved us for our worries, has made the modern industry of a few large firms an excellent instrument for inducing technical change'.[4]

This 'concentration effect' was tested by Professor Almarin Phillips. Using changes in the productivity of labour and in horse-power per employee as indicators of technical change, he found that in the United States from 1899 to 1939 industries with high concentration or large factories did have a greater rate of technical change and that this was not due to differences in the rate of increase of output.[5] Carter and Williams tested the concentration hypothesis for the United Kingdom, 1907–48, and found a correlation coefficient of 0·57 between the degree of concentration and the increase in product per man-hour. Between size of establishment and the increase in P M H the correlation coefficient was only 0·34. They concluded that 'neither the virtues and vices of small-firm industries have made much mark on the productivity of labour'.[6]

Even a perfect statistical correlation between concentration and innovation would not prove that the concentration had induced the technical change. The contrary relationship might hold and this (as well as the fairly low statistical correlation) should temper the temptation to jump to the conclusion that in any multi-firm industry, concentration would induce a greater rate of technical change. The *main* reason why some industries spend little on R and D is that the apparent opportunities for profitable R and D are small. This is the essence of the common distinction between the science-based and other industries. In the science-based industries research pays. But where production technology is based on art rather than on science, the opportuntities for profitable R and D in individual firms are much slighter. The similarity between the United Kingdom and the United States patterns of R and D is very striking (Table 1).

TABLE 1

Research and Development as Percentage of Net Output, 1958

	US companies	UK companies
Aircraft	30·9	35·1
Electronics	22·4	12·3
Other electrical	16·3	5·6
Vehicles	10·2	1·4
Instruments	9·9	6·0
Chemicals	6·9	4·5
Machinery	6·3	2·3
Rubber	2·7	2·1
Non-ferrous metals	2·0	2·3
Metal products	1·3	0·8
Stone, clay and glass	1·2	0·6
Paper	0·9	0·8
Ferrous metals	0·8	0·5
Food	0·5	0·3
Lumber and furniture	0·2	0·1
Textiles and apparel	0·2	0·3
All industries	5·7	3·1

Source: *National Institute Economic Review*, May 1962.

Differences in growth rates and the association between high growth rates and research are also very striking (Table 2). The correlation coefficient is 0·93.

When, however, we look at output per man-hour, and at individual firms within broad industry groups the position changes significantly. The relationship between 'productivity' growth and R and D percentages by broad industry groups is shown in Table 3.

The differing experiences of individual firms were analysed in *Industrial Research in Manufacturing Industry 1959–60*, (Federation of British Industries, 1961) conducted by Mr Freeman and Mr Evely of the National Institute of Economic and Social Research for the FBI. Freeman and Evely posed the question whether the firms that spend relatively most on R and D are those which grow fastest or are

TABLE 2

	RandD as % of net output 1958*	Output 1958 1935 = 100
Aircraft	35·1	974
Electronics	12·8	503
Instruments	6·0	472
Other electrical	5·6	263
Chemicals	4·5	382
Machinery	2·3	309
Non-ferrous metals	2·3	265
Rubber	2·1	239
Vehicles	1·4	213
Metal products	0·8	233
Paper	0·8	148
Stone, clay and glass	0·6	134
Ferrous metals	0·5	199
Other manufacturing	0·4	123
Food	0·3	170
Textiles and apparel	0·3	116
Lumber and furniture	0·1	113

* 1958 figures are used.

Source: C. Freeman, 'Research and Development: A Comparison Between British and American Industry', *National Institute Economic Review*, May 1962.

the most profitable. They used two measures of growth: (i) the annual average increase in net assets 1949–59; and (ii) average annual increase in net tangible fixed assets 1949–59. The measure of profit was the average annual rate of return on capital employed 1949–59. The measures of RandD were (i) the internal expenditure on RandD per hundred employed, 1960, which they called the 'Internal Expenditure ratio', and (ii) the number of qualified scientists and engineers (QSE) engaged on RandD (the 'research ratio').

Their sample consisted of forty-four firms in general engineering, twenty-two firms in chemicals, twelve firms in electrical engineering and seventeen firms in steel.

A positive association between growth, profitability, and research ratios was found for extreme cases, but the association did not persist systematically throughout the whole range of firms. It appeared that the greater part of the differences between firms in rates of growth and profitability are due to other factors than differences in the

TABLE 3

Expenditure on Research and Development

Industry group	Index of output per man-hour 1959 (1954 = 100) (Lomax index)	Expenditure on R and D as a % of net output 1955 (DSIR estimates)		% increase in expenditure on R and D 1955–8	
	A	B	Ranking	C	Ranking
1. Motor vehicles and cycles	133	0·9	(10)		
2. All vehicles	127	11·3	(1)	34	(8)
3. Oil refining	122	7·5	(2)	91	(1)
4. Chemicals and allied industries	122	4·8	(3)	77	(3)
5. Other manufacturing	117	1·8	(6)	41	(7)
6. Manufacturing industry	113	3·5	(4)	54	(5)
7. China and earthenware	113	0·5	(16)		
8. Textiles, leather and clothing	111			34	(8)
9. Metal goods not elsewhere specified	110	0·8	(12)		
10. Engineering, electrical goods, shipbuilding and marine engineering	109	3·5	(5)	80	(2)
11. Food, drink and tobacco	109	0·6	(14)	62	(4)
12. Paper and printing	109	0·5	(16)		
13. China and earthenware, glass, bricks and cement, etc.	109	1·0	(8)	21	(11)
14. Textiles	108	1·0	(8)		
15. Ferrous metal manufacture	108			27	(11)
16. Metal manufacture	107	0·9	(10)		
17. Non-ferrous metals	107	1·4	(7)	50	(6)
18. Paper and printing, timber and furniture	107			20	(12)
19. Bricks and cement, etc.	104	0·6	(14)		
20. Timber and furniture	104	0·2	(18)		
21. Leather, leather goods and fur	102	0·6	(14)		

The rank correlation coefficients are 0·63 between Columns A and B, and 0·46 between Columns A and C.

amount of R and D. The correlation coefficients (*r*) are shown in Table 4.

Of course when looking for possible causal relations between research and growth we need research ratios for an earlier period. Freeman and Evely did, in fact, get from a relevant group of firms research ratios in 1950 and found that the result was unaffected.

These results differ greatly from Minasion's for the United States chemical industry. Minasion found that the relevant R and D

TABLE 4

Correlation Coefficients for Research and Development and Growth or Profitability
The significant correlations are underlined.

	General engineering	Electrical engineering	Chemicals	Steel
Number of firms analysed	44	13	22	17
Internal expenditure ratio: Annual increase in net assets, 1949–59	0·04	0·39	0·33	0·13
Annual increase in net tangible fixed assets, 1949–59	0·13	0·29	0·26	0·27
Annual average return on capital employed, 1949–59	0·07	<u>0·56</u>	0·26	0·14
QSE engaged on R and D ratio Annual increase in net assets, 1949–59	0·11	0·41	0·39	0·13
Annual increase in net tangible fixed assets, 1949–59	<u>0·42</u>	0·24	0·22	0·13
Annual average return on capital employed, 1949–59	0·04	0·67	0·32	0·23
Significant value of '*r*' at 5% level	0·29	0·55	0·42	0·48

Source: *Industrial Research in Manufacturing Industry 1959–60*, p. 45.

expenditure was a highly significant independent variable explaining not only the rate of growth in productivity but also the trend of the profitability of eighteen chemical firms in the sample.[7] Because of the different levels of technology and the scientific manpower percentage, higher correlations between R and D and profits are more likely in the United States than in the United Kingdom.

Furthermore, it is necessary to take into account that there is a chain of relations between research, development, investment decisions, and final application, and that in any chain there may be a weak link or links. There is no reason to believe that a company's standard of performance in all areas of management – research, development, financial, production, marketing – is the same. The mere quantity of industrial research is by no means an infallible guide to growth potential. Industrial research will not create growth potential unless (i) the right problems are chosen, (ii) solved, and (iii) taken through the later stages of development and application. The choice of problems is critical and involves much more than a judgement from the researchers that a problem is interesting and

G

likely to produce a solution. It must be a problem relevant to the production and marketing situation and the management and financial capacity of the firm.

In *Industry and Technical Progress* (Chapter 6) Carter and I found it necessary to distinguish between 'fully considered', 'elliptical', and 'topsy' decisions. 'In a *fully considered* decision a company examines the R and D tasks to be performed to maintain the processes and products of the company on a competitive basis or to achieve some chosen growth in turn over or profit. It then relates these tasks to the size of the research department and its capacity for efficient growth, and the cost of performing these tasks to the finance available. This kind of consideration is rare. We found it in less than 10% of the companies we visited.' The appropriate choice of problems is dependent on effective communication between the research, development, production, and marketing departments, and we found that effective communication depended on having scientists and engineers not only in R and D but also in production departments and in some cases in marketing departments.[8]

We found that the willingness to use R and D outputs, and, in many cases, the ability to use new technologies, was also dependent on employing a sufficient number of scientists and engineers outside R and D. In other words, making good use of science in industry requires a balanced deployment of scientific manpower within the firm, and we judged that less than 10% of firms were in this position.

Industries are also very differently placed in their opportunities to profit from the technical changes of other industries (or countries). The railway industry did not invent the diesel engine; the vehicles industry played a small part in the invention of automatic transfer machines; the jet engine was invented by Whittle working outside the aircraft industry and receiving practically no support from it; the farming industry does little research but has much done for it.

The complex relation between technology and size is very clearly shown in the case of agriculture. Here in a good many countries, small firms have been able to make big changes in productivity because of public provision for research. Research has been concentrated, but not the industry. Agriculture helps in another way to point the complexity of the relation between technology and size. Because the separation of research and its application is relatively easy in agriculture, the isolated socialization of research is no barrier to the achievement of an optimum level of R and D. Yet even in Australia, which has a very distinguished record in this field, agricultural research is only 0·7% of agricultural net output (see Chapter VIII). How much more in the social interest any *industry* could spend on R and D is not something that can be decided for an industry subtracting its research rate from the research rates of science based industries (which in any case, as can be seen from Table 1, are quite widely dispersed).

3. OPPORTUNITY AND PRESSURE

The Marxian theory that innovation is an increasing function of the pressure of numbers is unsatisfactory; its opposite that innovation is an increasing function of the degree of concentration (possibly up to some critical limit[9]) is also unsatisfactory. What now of the possibility that competitive pressure to innovate is a function not of the number of firms but of the opportunities to innovate? Would not the pressure to innovate be greater in industries of high rank in Table 1 – industries that are very conscious of the many opportunities to innovate – than in industries of low rank? This suggestion is consistent with the position adopted by Schumpeter in his treatment of 'creative destruction', and there is a good deal of evidence to support the view that competition between the few in high-research industries is likely to be much more effective than competition between the many in low-research industries.* If we recast the pressure theory in terms not of the number of competitors but of effective pressure, it fits the facts rather better, though it lacks explanatory value to the extent that pressure is itself a function of opportunity. (I have examined this issue more fully in Chapter VI.)

Yet a purely opportunity theory of innovation which treats pressure as a simple function of opportunity is unsatisfactory. It implies that a highly concentrated science-based industry could never or would never operate a restrictive agreement on research and innovation and it implies that businessmen never need pressure to seek and identify opportunities to innovate. It is unlikely to be true that highly concentrated industries could never work a restrictive agreement on research and innovation. Some industries, e.g. glass, have no incentive to do this because of the obvious danger of competition from other industries, but this need not be true of all industries, and certainly not true of any industry at all times. Nor are all opportunities to innovate obvious. If they were, R and D would not be needed. But

---

* This is not meant to imply a demonstrable untruth that all high-research industries are concentrated and all low-research industries unconcentrated.

even with R and D there is an element of truth in the old saw that 'necessity is the mother of invention'. The process of industrial R and D requires for its effectiveness the 'discipline of the market'. In any research establishment there are hundreds of possible research problems. The most difficult problem is to identify those few that are most likely to issue in profitable innovations. Unless there is a strong pressure, and pressure on profit margins may be as good as any, the researchers may concentrate on what are to them the most interesting research problems. If so they may fail to identify and make ready opportunities for profitable innovation.

Technological opportunities to innovate are a necessary condition of effective competitive pressure, but they are not a sufficient condition. It is therefore sensible to list both pressure and opportunity as conditions of rapid innovation. It is however not possible to generalize about the sufficient conditions to pressure. The definition of an industry is usually rather arbitrary and although there may not be much competition within an industry there may be intense competition between the products of different industries. Building materials provide a good example. It is also difficult to generalize about the necessary conditions. The opportunity to innovate may be provided by supplying industries (such as, for example, the makers of machine tools), by other industries with similar processes, by similar industries in other countries (perhaps on licence), or by internal research and/or development departments. In some industries the generation of opportunities to innovate may require a large R and D effort that only large firms can afford; in other industries the appropriate research and/or development effort may be manageable to quite small companies. In some industries the provision and use of opportunities to innovate may be separated (as in agriculture); in other industries the appropriate R and D must be tied pretty closely to the production facilities and problems of the firms concerned. In other words to know the conditions most likely to encourage innovation we must study the problem industry by industry. In this as in so many problems of applied economics there is, in the expression of the old Chinese proverb, no substitute for sweat.

REFERENCES

1. J. A. SCHUMPETER, *Capitalism, Socialism and Democracy,*

2nd ed. (Allen & Unwin, 1950), p. 104. See also J. K. GAL-BRAITH, *American Capitalism* (Hamilton, 1957).

2. See, for example, P. WILES, 'Growth versus Choice', *Economic Journal* (June 1956).
3. *Capitalism, Socialism and Democracy* (see ref. 1), p. 106.
4. *American Capitalism* (see ref. 1), p. 86.
5. *Journal of Industrial Economics*, June 1956.
6. C. F. CARTER and B. R. WILLIAMS, *Industry and Technical Progress* (Oxford University Press, 1957), p. 121.
7. 'The Economics of Research and Development', in *The Rate and Direction of Inventive Activity*, Princeton, 1962, pp. 93–142.
8. For a further development of this point see CARTER and WILLIAMS, *Science in Industry* (Oxford University Press, 1959), Part I.
9. Galbraith's position on this is ambiguous. See *American Capitalism* (ref. 1), Chapter 7.

VIII

Industrial Research and
Economic Growth in Australia*

Alfred North Whitehead once wrote that the greatest invention of the nineteenth century was the invention of the art of invention. He anticipated many later writers who have claimed this invention for our time. But whenever, if ever, the art of invention was invented, there is no doubt the use of science in agriculture and industry has made a profound difference to our lives. It has brought a truly remarkable increase in food and population, exciting new processes such as atomic power stations and computer-controlled machines and plants, and an extraordinary array of new drugs, man-made fibres, TV, radar, jet aircraft, moon rockets, and bombs that could end it all.

In the short time that I have been back in Australia, I have read and heard much of the need for more research. Australian expenditure on research is often compared very unfavourably with that in the United Kingdom and the United States. Whereas the United Kingdom and the United States spend more than 2% of their GNPs on R and D, Australia is said to spend little more than one-half of 1%; and whereas the United Kingdom spends over 3% of net industrial output on purely industrial R and D, Australian industry, it is said, spends a mere quarter of 1% and most of that on 'development rather than research'.[1]

It is usually taken for granted that not keeping up with the United Kingdom and the United States is a sign of 'backwardness'. To say, in this context, that Australia is backward implies that spending a higher proportion of national product on R and D would ensure a higher rate of economic growth; and Dr Encel's comment, which reflects the views of many scientists in universities and research organizations, that Australian industry spends very little on R and D and that 'almost all of this is development rather than research'

* The 30th Joseph Fisher Lecture in Commerce, University of Adelaide, 24th July, 1962.

implies that to increase the rate of economic growth special attention should be given to research.

In this lecture I will not take all this for granted. Instead I will examine whether these judgements are based on the available evidence. Is it true that Australian economic growth could be increased by spending a higher proportion of national product on R and D? Is there a special deficiency in research expenditure? In an attempt to answer these questions, I will first define the terms involved, and then examine the expenditure on various types of R and D.

I. HOW MUCH RESEARCH?

Research is the activity of extending the bounds of scientific knowledge. *Basic research* is concerned with fundamental scientific problems, which may be quite unrelated to the current problems of industry, agriculture, medicine, and defence; by contrast, *applied research* is concerned with application to such current problems. Such applied research may be short-term and direct. It may, however, be *background* applied and difficult to distinguish from basic research, as suggested by a research worker in a large industrial laboratory who remarked that 'if you want me to do it, it's applied; if I want to do it myself, it's basic'. *Development*, the process of appraising the results of research, of selecting the most promising, and of making them ready for actual application in industry, includes the process of building and testing pilot plants or prototypes. *Application* or *innovation* is the process of adopting a development and of getting it to perform as it was designed to perform, or better. It is only this final step that gives us the new or improved products or processes. It is therefore this final process of innovation that counts in growth.

In Australia, Government research agencies dominate the field. The Department of Supply conducts Defence Standards Laboratories, Weapons Research Establishments, and Aeronautical Research Laboratories for military R and D, costing more than £12 million a year. The Commonwealth Scientific and Industrial Research Organization is concerned with civil R and D over a very wide field, ranging from basic research in such things as genetics and radio astronomy, to development work in textile technology and rain-making. It now spends more than £10 million a year. Other Commonwealth Government agencies – the Atomic Energy Commission, the Commonwealth Health Department, the Bureau of Mineral Resources, the Bureau of Meteorology, the Forestry and Timber Bureau, and the Ionospheric Prediction Service – spend another £7–8 million on research.

Universities play a small but important part in research. Their research is mostly basic, and the conduct of this research is usually associated with the training of high-grade research workers. Because of this, and of the other teaching duties of professors and lecturers, estimates of spending on research in universities depend in some measure on assumptions made about the proportion of time that members of staff devote to research. Recent estimates of university research have ranged from £3 million to £5 million.

There is a notable lack of information about R and D in industry. In 1955 the Research Survey Committee of the Institution of Engineers inquired into the amount of *industrial* research but as the response was poor it could only conclude that '104 firms with production in excess of £500 million spent £1·7 million'.[2] Two investigators from the Stanford Research Institute recently blew up this estimate to allow for incomplete response, for later salary increases, and for the subsequent growth of secondary industry, and they concluded that in 1960 industrial research was £15 million.[3] By contrast Dr Encel used the same original estimate, but after inquiries in BHP and the Colonial Sugar Refining Company decided that

Two Estimates of Research and Development
£ million

	Encel 1958–9	Stanford 1959–60
CSIRO	8·5	9·2
Supply Department	11·7	(12·5)*
AAEC	2·7	3·8
Other Commonwealth Government	4·5	2·5
State Governments	2·5	2·0
Universities	4·0	3·0
Industry	3·0–5·0	15·0
	37–39	48
% of GNP	0·6	0·7

* The Stanford estimate excluded defence. I have added the figure in parentheses to make the two estimates comparable.

it could be 'said with some assurance that the total amount spent in 1958–9 did not exceed £5 million'.[4]

We have no reason to trust either 'guesstimate' of industrial research. To get a check I have tried an alternative approach by way of the manpower statistics of the Department of Labour.[5] These statistics are not very satisfactory – they were built up from a purely voluntary register, the definitions of qualified scientists and engineers were loose, and the interpretation of RandD activity was far from strict – but more satisfactory information from CSIRO and the Department of Supply makes possible some necessary adjustments.

The unadjusted Department of Labour statistics imply that 8,000 scientsts and engineers were engaged in non-university RandD in 1959 – one-third of this number in 'industry'. Now we know the expenditure on RandD in CSIRO and the number of qualified scientists and engineers (as usually defined). From these we can deduce the cost of RandD per qualified CSIRO scientist or engineer. This was £6,800 in 1959. In the Department of Supply the comparable cost was about £10,000. If we use an average figure of £8,000 for Government RandD, the implication is that approximately 3,750 qualified scientists and engineers were employed on RandD. Using the Department of Labour ratio of industrial to Government employment, we arrive at a figure of approximately 1,900 qualified scientists and engineers employed in industrial RandD. In the United Kingdom the cost per qualified industrial RandD man was at this time just under £8,000. We do not know the figure for Australia, though from the few inquiries that I have been able to make it appears to have been in the region of £4,500–£5,000. If so, the cost of industrial RandD done by the 1,900 qualified scientists and engineers was between £8½ and £9½ million. This estimate is almost the average of the Encel and Stanford estimates. This is an accident from which I derive no comfort or assurance. My estimate is based on 'informed guessing', which is a beguiling but often misleading activity. However, the knowledge that in the seven large firms that are frequently named when industrial research is discussed the expenditure is near £5 million, makes me hope that my guess will prove to be 'informed'.

Recently Mr L. Weickhardt[6] argued that if we make proper allowance for the small number of large companies in Australia it is unrealistic to expect Australian industry to spend more than £7 million on RandD. However, this estimate is based on the assumption that the minimum cost of an effective RandD department is £100,000 per annum. This may be true of the chemical industry, but it is not true generally; and in any case there will be many firms engaged only in development work.

2. THE NATURE OF AUSTRALIAN RESEARCH AND DEVELOPMENT

The overall position in R and D is that the Government effort costs £30 million, the university effort, say, £5 million, the industrial effort, say, £9 million. It is clear that Government agencies dominate the field. Defence accounts for more than 40% of Government R and D. Commonwealth Government expenditure on the peaceful development of atomic energy, medical research, research into forestry, timber and mineral resources, and State-Government research in agriculture account for another one-quarter of the Government effort, and the remaining 30% is provided by CSIRO.

In the civil field, both Government and private, CSIRO is the dominant organization. Fortunately it publishes a good deal of information about the nature of its activities. Until 1938, when defence problems pushed it into a range of industrial research, CSIRO's research was centred on primary industry. After the war when defence research was transferred to other Government agencies, the reconstituted CSIRO did not take the occasion to 'go bush' again. In 1960–1 CSIRO's research budget was £10 million. £5½ million of this went on R and D related to primary industries. The other £4½ million was spread over chemical research (almost £1 million), the National Standards Laboratory (£848,000), Radio Physics (£500,000), Meteorological Physics (£128,000), Wool-Textile Technology (£450,000), Coal Technology (£280,000), Building (£207,000), and a range of smaller items. The expenditure that was consciously directed to the needs of Australian industry was in the region of £2½ million.

To the CSIRO expenditure of £2½ million on secondary industry R and D, we can add industry's own expenditure of £8½–9½ million. This total of £11–12 million was approximately 0·6% of the net value of secondary production in 1959.

Primary industry R and D in CSIRO, in other Commonwealth, and in State research organizations, was approximately £9 million. This was 0·7% of the net value of primary production in 1959.

To go further and to break down these civil figures into basic research, applied research, and development involves a deal of guessing. However, CSIRO publications such as *Research Review* and *Annual Report* make possible informed guessing about the main civil spender. Let us start by allocating to basic research all the university expenditure of £5 million. Basic research in CSIRO appears to cost about £4½ million; in AAEC it may be £1 million. Total expenditure on basic research, then, is £10–11 million.

In applied research CSIRO spends £3½ million and State Government and other Commonwealth agencies £3½ million. AAEC spends £2½–3 million and industry £2–3 million. Total expenditure on applied research, then, appears to be in the region of £11–12 million.

On development, industry spends £6–7 million, CSIRO £1 million, and other Government agencies £2 million – a total of £9–10 million.

These estimates are necessarily rough and are meant only to indicate the order of the problem. The Australian civil R and D effort appears to be fairly evenly distributed between basic research, applied research, and development. The cost of each of these activities is a little less than the cost of military R and D.

After this outline of the facts of the situation, so far as I have been able to establish them, I came on to the teasing problems of evaluation. Is the overall expenditure too low? Is there a sensible distribution of effort between primary and secondary industry? Is there an appropriate balance between R and D? These are the critical questions to which we would all like the answers. I wish that it were possible to give them, but in the present state of knowledge of Australian conditions it is easier to expose the wrong answers than to provide the correct ones. Still, this is something; and I hope to go further and indicate the appropriate lines of further inquiry.

3. STATISTICAL RELATIONS BETWEEN RESEARCH AND GROWTH

It is important to emphasize that there is no established statistical link between research and growth. The United Kingdom and the United States devote a relatively high proportion of their national products to R and D but they have not achieved notably high rates of growth. The Australian rate of growth in real product per man-hour has been higher than the British despite its much lower ratio of R and D to output. Nor in the United Kingdom and the United States has there been any apparent acceleration in the rate of economic growth with the post-war acceleration of growth in R and D. It is not possible to provide simple statistical evidence that it would pay Australia to raise its ratio of research to output. The bald assertion that Australian industry is backward because it spends a small portion of net output on research, reminds me of Belloc's jibe:

> The scientists who ought to know
> Assure us that it must be so;
> Oh, let us never, never doubt,
> What nobody is sure about.

In fact the lack of a close statistical relationship between research and growth should not be a matter of surprise. The use of science in industry depends on research, on development and on application, as previously defined. But these are not measured and successive steps required for each innovation.

In some innovations, basic research, applied research, development and application, do appear as measured and successive steps. Thus Rutherford's atom-splitting experiments were followed a short time later by applied research on atomic fission, by development work on making bombs, and by the industrial application of the results of this R and D. But this is by no means a typical case. J. J. Thomson's basic research on electrons also provided, in the end, for a new industry, but the time lag was fifty years and there was not an orderly sequence of events from research to application.

Just as a contemporary innovation may draw on the basic or applied research of an earlier generation, so it may draw on the research work of another country. Sir Alexander Fleming's original observation on penicillin mould in 1928 was the starting point for Florey's work between 1938 and 1942. Although Florey was able to produce enough penicillin for clinical trials, the high-yield methods of growth suitable for commercial exploitation were developed in the United States. The original work on silicones was done by 1908 by Kipping of Nottingham; the development and application between 1932 and 1942 was the work of the Corning Glass Works of America and The Dow Chemical Company. Most of the applied R and D leading to the atom bomb took place in North America; after the war, the United Kingdom built on this and developed the first atomic power stations.

It is quite possible for a country to provide more than its share of the world's scientific output but less than its share of development and innovation. This, it is often said, is the position in the United

Kingdom: 'The United Kingdom invents, foreigners apply.'
Although this is a conceit that the United Kingdom shares with
other nations, it is true that if there were not a 'development gap'
United Kingdom science would have a much bigger impact on
United Kingdom industry.[7] Research may be relatively inefficient in
generating growth because it is not followed through to the point of
application. This follow-through is by no means simple, as we shall
see.

Another country might produce less than its share of science
but more than its share of development. Until fairly recently this was
true of the United States. Other countries could decide to do little
about either research or development and to concentrate on the
effective application of foreign developed processes and products.
This is a development gap in reverse. Switzerland followed this policy
until the 1930's, and in some measure Japan follows it still. Australia
in its reliance on branches or subsidiaries of foreign companies, has
acquired growth from the United Kingdom and United States'
R and D. We can call this Australia's vicarious research. If in our
foreign dominated industries such as chemicals and vehicles, R and D
was the relevant United Kingdom percentage of net output (less
present Australian percentage in these industries), industrial R and D
would be £15–20 million more than the actual £9 million. This gives
a rough idea of the importance of vicarious R and D in the Australian
economy.

The links between a country's growth and its R and D expenditure
are also complicated by military affairs. In 1958 the United Kingdom
spent 2·3% of net output on R and D. However, more than one-half of
this total expenditure was for defence R and D.[8] The position in
the United States was very similar. Some defence R and D yields
civil benefit, but by no means all.

4. THE USES OF SCIENTIFIC MANPOWER

I have already mentioned that the follow-through from research to
application provides complex problems. It is obvious that scientists
and engineers are needed for industrial R and D. They are also
needed for the actual application of science to industrial processes.
In the chemical industry in the United Kingdom, qualified scientists
and engineers make up 3·7% of the total labour force, though only
one-third of them are engaged in R and D. In aircraft, electrical
engineering, and precision instruments, only one-half of the

scientists and engineers are employed on R and D work. For the whole economy, 40% of the qualified scientists and engineers were engaged on R and D. The final application of science to industry often cannot take place unless scientific manpower is employed for the control of production processes. When even the day-to-day operation of sophisticated industrial processes requires highly qualified technologists, the successful introduction of new processes in factories is likely to be still more dependent on them. The use of science in industry has very much reduced the usefulness of production men 'qualified only by experience'.

The need not to concentrate scientific manpower in R and D is increased by the problem of identifying the relevant lines of research. Efficiency in industrial research is largely a matter of choosing the right problems. There are thousands upon thousands of possible research projects – the crucial task is to choose those few projects which are made relevant by the market position, the financial resources, the production problems, and the management skills of the firm. Unless the research workers are guided by experts in production, costing, finance, and marketing, they are unlikely to identify the promising lines of research; they are more likely to tangle their feet in the clouds. Perhaps Mark Spade had this in mind when in *Business for Pleasure* he sardonically advised directors to: 'Give the Research Department only Big, Long-Term Problems and leave the results in trust for your heirs.

It follows that there is an important problem of finding an efficient distribution of scientific manpower between teaching, basic research, applied research, development, application, control of production processes, and technical selling. It is quite possible to impede the application of science to industry by drawing scientists into research and so impoverishing activities in development and production departments. Since the purpose of applied R and D is presumably to generate innovations in industry and agriculture, it is usually better to think in terms of the overall use of scientific manpower and not simply in terms of money spent on research. In some circumstances more research means less growth.

5. THE SPECIAL PROBLEMS OF RESEARCH IN AUSTRALIA

The number of qualified scientists and engineers in Australia is small, both in number and as a percentage of the population.* It

* As a percentage of population the Australian supply of scientists and engineers appears to be 60% of the U K figure.

follows that it would be foolish to spread our R and D efforts as widely as, say, the United Kingdom does. It follows too, that in some fields it may pay us to rely on the research and/or the development work of other countries. This sets a problem in identification. In which fields should we rely on others; in which should we concentrate our efforts?

Let us start with defence. In both the United Kingdom and the United States defence R and D absorbs a large part of the scientific manpower. This is a field in which size really matters; a field on which we could not hope to make much of an impression. At most it could be sensible to take on a few marginal problems to complement the work of allied countries. The Weapons Research Establishment, operating at Salisbury and Woomera, which co-operates with the United Kingdom's Ministry of Defence, is an example of such a complementary effort. The Australian defence research effort at 30% of the total spending on R and D uses a significantly smaller percentage of scientific manpower than do the United Kingdom and United States efforts. Given the low level of scientific manpower in Australia this seems wise.

In primary industry, there are special problems set by climate and soil. We cannot rely on the research of others, and primary industry, with a net value of production of over £1,200 million, is big enough to justify a substantial effort in both R and D. There is in fact a substantial effort. In 1959 the expenditure was £9 million, 0·7% of the net value of primary production. I know of no way of deducing from these figures whether we ought to be spending more, and I do not know enough about either the detail of the research effort or the problems of application to judge whether the R and D resources have been deployed in the best way. My general impression is that the resources have been deployed well, but a definite answer to this question requires a more careful joint scientific and economic appraisal of research programmes and their results than CSIRO, and State Departments of Agriculture or independent researchers have given them.

In secondary industries the problems of applying science are both more complex and less special than in agriculture. They are more complex in the sense that the isolated socialization of research is likely to be less efficient than in primary industry. The range of output is much less in wheat or wool or dairy farms than in engineering or chemical or electrical factories. And, because so much less of the actual production can be left to nature, the dependence on scientific manpower is generally greater within factories than on farms. R and D isolated from production is therefore generally less successful in secondary than in primary industry. The problems are less special in the sense that our raw materials and climate do not render irrelevant much of the research work of other countries. This is fortunate, because any attempt to cover the whole field would lead to the growth of many inefficiently small and ineffective research departments and to a drain of scientific manpower out of other important work. (I assume, I think realistically, that the increased demand for scientific manpower would not be met by increased imports from abroad.) In development, too, the work of other countries is generally relevant, though there are some special problems of adapting foreign techniques to Australian climate, raw materials, and cost structure.

It does not follow from the fact that our problems are not for the most part special, that it must pay us to ignore industrial research. In some fields it will pay us, in others not. In some fields the cost of buying knowhow may be so high that it would be more economical to develop our own technologies. The cost of buying knowhow tends to be high in the 'patent sensitive fields' in which, it so happens, small countries can sometimes compete with the big: witness the success of Switzerland in pharmaceuticals and dyes, and Holland in electronics. Where our universities and research institutes make significant contributions to basic research in the relevant 'patent sensitive' fields, we can expect to find opportunities for profitable industrial R and D.

It is, however, misleading to think of R and D as the general alternative to buying knowhow. Often the relevant alternative will be between spending money on development or on buying knowhow. Given that the objective is the fruitful *application* of science to industry it is reasonable to assume that it would be wise for a country with a special shortage of scientific manpower (in the sense already explained) to concentrate more of its manpower near the point of application than in countries with a less acute shortage. In other words, we should expect Australian industrial R and D to be more concentrated on development than in say the United Kingdom or the United States, unless a range of Australian industry is made so dependent on foreign technology that there ceases to be a shortage of scientific manpower to deal with the problems of the other industries. As I have indicated in my calculation of vicarious research, certain Australian industries, notably chemicals and vehicles, do draw considerably on foreign R and D. But this does not keep them out of the market for scientific manpower. The vehicles industry uses engineers for local development and for production; the chemical industry is a large employer of scientists and engineers for research, development and production.

Looked at in this way the roughly equal distribution of expenditure between basic research, applied R and D does not look ideal. Even by comparison with the United States – a large economy with a relatively good supply of scientific manpower – the ratios of applied to basic research and of development to applied research are low. For industry alone, development expenditure is approximately equal to the total of relevant basic and applied research, which again by comparison with the industrial sector even in large countries suggests that development is very low in relation to research.

There is another problem that calls for further investigation. A high percentage of expenditure on research relevant to industry is conducted by institutions with no direct interests in production and selling. There is evidence from other countries that does not encourage a rapid application of science to industry.[9] Research detached from production problems and facilities is quite likely to increase the sum of unused applied science; to add to the development gap. In primary industry, CSIRO for example has experimental farms and is able to develop the results of its research under field conditions. In part of its coal research it is able to find solutions to particular problems referred to it by industry. In textile technology it has created production facilities to carry through its development work on processing and finishing to the point of application. But elsewhere CSIRO has not given such attention to the problem of the development gap. Part of this problem must remain unsolved until manufacturers employ a sufficient number of scientists and technologists to make possible a fruitful collaboration, but even so I suspect that CSIRO is not giving sufficient attention to the choice of fields in which it could make its biggest contribution to Australian industry. I do not pretend to know what these fields are. The knowledge cannot be acquired without a considerable joint research effort by economists and scientists.*

* It is interesting to note that the role of research associations in Australia has been small. There are research associations for bread, wine, coal, and tobacco, but the total expenditure is very small – it is about one-twentieth of what it would be if we used research associations as they are used in the United Kingdom for co-operative research in industries where there are many small firms.

H

6. THE ROLE OF OVERSEAS COMPANIES

I referred earlier to the importance of vicarious RandD. I have argued that these foreign companies do not relieve Australia of its special shortage of scientific manpower. But do they overcome the apparent under-emphasis on development? This is an important question. Australian subsidiaries or branches of overseas companies can draw on the results of RandD that costs very much more than £15–20 million, and, more importantly, they draw on the successful results. It is therefore reasonable to treat most of this vicarious expenditure as equivalent to development. It is this operation of overseas companies that begins to make sense of the Australian use of scientific manpower. I put the matter in this way quite deliberately. Much of the argument about the need for more research in Australia arises from the belief that we spend too much on buying foreign knowhow. Significantly, and shamefully, we do not know how much is spent, but even if we did, the fact would remain that we lack the scientific manpower to be self-sufficient in our technology, and that the more we tried to be, the more it would be necessary in the interests of economic growth (though not necessarily of scientific fun) to put more money into development rather than research.

At the beginning of this lecture I quoted Dr Encel's estimate that Australian industry spends a mere quarter of 1% of net industrial output on RandD. If Australian industry spent the same percentage as United Kingdom industry, industrial RandD would cost £70 million. Such a comparison, though it is often used, is rendered meaningless by the different structures of the two countries. The United Kingdom weights are wrong for Australian conditions. If instead of using the United Kingdom average net industrial output on RandD, we use the appropriate percentage for each industry – 36% for aircraft, 12% for electronics, 6% for chemicals, one-quarter of 1% for wood paper and pulp, and so on – then the comparable figure for Australia is not £70 million but something like £40 million. (The eccentric way in which Australian production statistics are compiled makes an accurate estimate impossible.) If to the direct Australian industrial expenditure of (the calculated) £9 million we add the vicarious expenditure of £15–20 million (and, in the interests of realism, some such addition should be made to the direct expenditure) the Australian effort does not look quite so puny.

In saying this I do not want to give the impression that there is good reason for complacency. The special shortage of scientific manpower is in part due to a low ratio of scientific to total manpower. If this ratio is raised the opportunities to make and to use science will be increased. And though I have stressed the very important role of overseas companies I have not implied that we do get the benefits of these companies on the most favourable terms. Indeed I do not think that we do, and I think it high time that more attention was given both to the capital structure and to the limited trading opportunities of the Australian parts of overseas companies. These are distinct issues, however.

7. SUMMARY AND CONCLUSIONS

(*a*) The relation between research and growth is complex. Growth in output per head depends on new or improved products and processes of production. The life history of such innovations is made up of the *basic research* from which *applied research* grows, the *development* of the results of applied research to prepare them for use in production, the *decision* to use the new development or design and where necessary to *invest* in the planned innovation, the *application* of the new method to the farm or the factory processes, and the *marketing* of any new products which in some cases involves sophisticated technical selling and service.

(*b*) These events in the life history of innovations do not usually follow each other in a consistent time sequence. Nor need all these events take place in the same industry, or in the same country. In any country, the life history may start with research or with development or with application.

(*c*) All these events in the life history of innovation depend in some measure on the use of scientific manpower. R and D depend on the employment of scientists and engineers. So, too, does the actual introduction of the new method to the farm or the factory – whether in the form of field officers or production engineers. Sometimes *operating* the new processes is fairly simple and only calls for occasional servicing by experts; frequently, as in a chemical plant, day-to-day operation depends on highly qualified technologists. The use of science in industry has very much reduced the usefulness of those 'qualified only by experience'.

(*d*) It is misleading to think of the possible contributions of science to industry just in terms of research, or even in terms of R and D. It is possible to have too much research. It is possible to produce many more useful scientific ideas than can be developed and applied by the scientists and engineers employed in development and production. It is also possible to have too much research in another sense, namely, that a higher rate of innovation could be achieved by using a higher proportion of a country's scientific manpower to develop and/or apply the research results of other countries. In other words, it is possible to aim for an inefficiently high level of self-sufficiency in research as well as in production. The key problem is not how much applied research, but how best to distribute the scientific manpower between research, development and other activities. Much of the talk about the need for more and more research implies either that there is an unlimited supply of scientists and engineers, or that they are only good for R and D work.

(*e*) It is not possible to speak with confidence (at any rate, not possible for me to speak with confidence) about the precise balance of the Australian effort. The information on which such a judgement should be based is often conspicuous by its absence. However, such calculations as I have been able to make lead me to suspect that Australian industry is backward in its use, or lack of use, of qualified scientists and engineers for both production and development. I suspect also that too high a proportion of the applied research effort is too detached from production interests and development facilities. Such remoteness usually leads to a mixture of irrelevance in applied science and of failure to bridge the gaps between invention and innovation. Such remoteness is therefore likely to impede growth.

(*f*) To get to the answers to these questions we need accurate information on R and D expenditure in industry and on the size and distribution of scientific manpower. We need research into possible lines of innovation that look promising on both scientific and economic grounds, into the problems of distributing scientific manpower efficiently, into the cost of making innovations at home compared to the cost of buying them from abroad. These are important and interesting lines of research, and I take this occasion to express surprise that so very few resident Australian scientists, both natural and social, have found them so. If this lecture should help in any way to stimulate such research, I should have some reason to think that I had done my duty to Joseph Fisher.

REFERENCES

1. S. ENCEL, 'Financing Scientific Research in Australia', *Science* (28th July, 1961).
2. Institution of Engineers, *Australian Industrial Research* (1955).
3. Stanford Research Institute, *Applied Research on the Development of Australia* (1960).
4. As ref. 1.
5. Australian Department of Labour Reports on *The Employment of Scientists, The Employment of Engineers, The Employment of Chemists, The Employment of Physicists.*
6. 'The Future of Manufacturing Industry', a paper read at the Autumn Forum of the Victorian Branch of the Economic Society, to be published as a monograph by the Committee for Economic Development of Australia.
7. For an appraisal of this and related issues see C. F. CARTER and B. R. WILLIAMS, *Industry and Technical Progress* (Oxford University Press, 1957), Chapter 3.
8. Department of Scientific and Industrial Research, *Industrial Research and Development Expenditure* (1958).
9. C. F. CARTER and B. R. WILLIAMS, *Science in Industry* (Oxford University Press, 1959).

IX

Investment and Technology
in Growth*

Growth is a big and complex problem. Single factor explanations generally follow from simple-mindedness or ignorance of the facts. In this paper I have chosen to concentrate on two factors – investment and technology – not because I think we can explain growth that way, but because I must limit the growth of this paper. They do in any case provide an interesting set of problems. For at the very time when the investment rate has become a fundamental preoccupation of Governments concerned with economic growth, grave doubts have been raised about the historical growth role of investment as such.

I. THE INVESTMENT RATE APPROACH

Growth is sometimes treated as a simple function of the investment (or savings) rate. This approach was first explicitly used by Gustav Cassel.[1] He assumed the capital-output ratio to be a technologically determined constant. Where k is the (marginal) capital-output ratio and s the rate of saving, the percentage growth must be $(s/k) \times 100$. Cassel assumed that $k = 6$ and $s = \frac{1}{5}$ and concluded that the normal rate of growth in industrial societies is $3 \cdot 3\%$.

In this type of approach, to be found also in the Harrod-Domar growth models, a country's output increases at the same rate as its real capital. With k equal to 6, and a rate of saving equal to $0 \cdot 15$, growth rate is $2 \cdot 5$; raise s to $0 \cdot 2$ and growth rises to $3 \cdot 3$; raise s to $0 \cdot 25$ and growth rises to $4 \cdot 2$. This makes growth look easy. To get more growth we simply push up the investment rate. Small wonder that members of this school wait eagerly for the periodical publication of the investment league table.

That Cassel's guess about the normal growth rate of $3\frac{1}{3}\%$ proved to be wide of the mark can be seen from Tables 1 and 2.

* Revised version of a paper read to the Manchester Statistical Society, January 1964.

TABLE 1

Growth of Gross Domestic Product
(annual average compound growth-rate)

	1870–1955	1870–1913	1913–38	1938–55	1955–64
	%	%	%	%	%
Denmark	2·6	3·2	1·9	2·4	5·0
France	1·4	1·6	0·4	2·3	5·0
Germany	2·3*	2·9*	1·6	3·0	5·6
Italy	1·6	1·4	1·7	2·0	5·7
Japan	3·1†	3·3†	4·4	0·6	10·4
Norway	2·5*	2·2*	2·9	2·6	4·2
Sweden	2·6	3·0	1·8	3·2	4·3
UK	1·8	2·1	1·1	1·9	3·1
US	3·7*	4·3*	2·0	4·8	3·1
USSR	2·6	2·5	n.a.	n.a.	6·1‡

* Earliest figure 1871.
† Earliest figure 1879.
‡ 1955–63.
Source: Maddison, *Economic Growth in the West.*

TABLE 2

Growth of Output per Man Employed
(annual average compound growth-rate)

	1870–1955	1870–1913	1913–38	1938–55	1955–64
	%	%	%	%	%
Denmark	1·6	2·1	0·7	1·6	3·8
France	1·4	1·4	0·9	2·1	4·7
Germany	1·5*	1·6*	0·8	1·9	4·4
Italy	1·2	0·8	1·5	1·6	5·7
Japan	2·2†	2·4†	3·7	− 0·5	8·8
Norway	1·6*	1·4*	1·9	2·0	3·9
UK	1·0	1·0	0·7	1·2	2·6
US	1·8*	1·9*	1·2	2·4	1·9

* Earliest figure 1871.
† Earliest figure 1879.
Source: Maddison, *Economic Growth in the West.*

These differences in growth over time and between countries are not simply due to differences in investment rates. Chart 1 plots the relationship between growth rates and investment ratios in recent years. It is obvious from Chart 1 that, recently at least, there must have been large differences in incremental capital/output ratios between countries. The incremental capital/output ratios are given in Table 3.

Chart 1

*Percentage Rates of Growth of Domestic Product and Investment Ratios
in Western Countries, 1949–59*

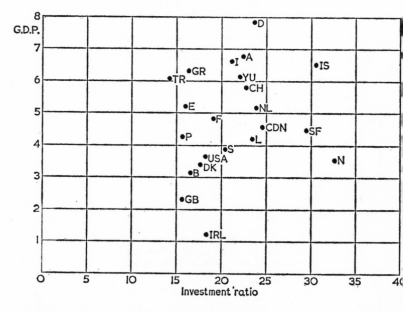

Key: A, Austria; B, Belgium; CDN, Canada; CH, Switzerland; D, Germany
(Federal Republic); DK Denmark; E, Spain; IRL, Eire; F, France; GB, United
Kingdom; GR, Greece; I, Italy; IS, Iceland; L, Luxembourg; N, Norway;
NL, Netherlands; P, Portugal; S, Sweden; SF, Finland; TR, Turkey; USA
United States; YU, Yugoslavia.

Source: *Economic Survey of Europe 1961* (UN).

One possible conclusion to be drawn from these relations between
growth and investment rates is that the productivity of investment
has played a much more important part than the investment rate in
determining differences in growth rates. This is the conclusion
drawn, for example, by Aukrust, who has argued that the rate of
growth which can be attained in a modern industrial economy is not
strongly influenced by investment policy, and that whether the
investment rate is high or low technical progress will ensure a growth
of about 1·5% per annum.[2]

TABLE 3

Incremental Gross Capital/Output Ratios, 1949–59

Country	Growth rates of GNP			Incremental capital/ output ratio
	Total GNP	GNP per capita	GNP per person employed	
	1	*2*	*3*	*4*
West Germany	7·5	6·4	5·2	3·3
Austria	6·1	5·9	5·8	3·9
Italy	5·9	5·4	4·3	3·7
Netherlands	4·9	3·6	3·4	5·2
France	4·3	3·4	3·9	4·6
Canada	3·9	1·2	1·9	6·0
Norway	3·5	2·5	3·2	9·5
Denmark	3·3	2·6	2·5	5·5
US	3·3	1·6	2·1	5·5
Sweden	3·2	2·6	2·9	6·3
Belgium	2·9	2·3	2·5	5·6
UK	2·6	2·2	2·0	6·7
Luxembourg	2·1	1·5	1·2	6·2
Ireland	1·4	1·9	2·5	13·7
Average 14 countries	3·9	3·1	3·1	6·1
Greece	6·2	5·3	—	3·0
Turkey	5·8	2·9	—	2·6
Switzerland	5·1	3·7	—	4·5
Spain	4·9	4·1	—	3·1
Iceland	4·8	2·7	—	5·7
Portugal	3·9	3·2	—	4·0
Average 20 countries	4·1	3·2	—	5·4

Source: *Economic Survey of Europe 1961*, Part II (UN), Table 6.

2. TECHNICAL PROGRESS

Appraisal of Aukrust's generalization requires the introduction of the Cobb-Douglas production function, which expresses a relationship between output (O) and the inputs of labour (L) and capital (C):

$$O = cL^aC^b$$

If a 1% increase of labour leads to an increase in output of $0·7\%$, and a 1% increase of capital to an increase in output of $0·3\%$, then the production function would be

$$O = cL^{0.7}C^{0.3}$$

If over time the increase in O proves greater than this formula leads us to expect, then a trend component, z, can be added to represent the annual percentage change in output due to 'technical progress' or 'the human factor'. Expressing the function in terms of annual percentage changes, we have

$$\frac{\Delta O}{O} = \frac{a\Delta L}{L} + \frac{b\Delta C}{C} + z$$

For the Norwegian economy 1900–55 Aukrust and Bjerke estimated the value of a as 0·76, of b as 0·20, and of z as 1·8.[3] For the United States 'private non-farm activity' for the years 1900–55, R. Solow estimated the value of a as 0·65, of b as 0·35, and of z as 1·5.[4] For West Germany 1925–57, Gehrig and Kuhlo estimated the value of a as 0·76, of b as 0·34, and of z as 1·9.[5]

For these three countries the values of a and b were not the same. If, however, these variations are ignored and standard values assumed for them, it becomes a simple matter to calculate for different countries the contributions to growth made by increases in labour and capital, and therefore the contribution of the residual factor z. On the assumption that $a = 0·7$ and $b = 0·3$ (which implies the absence of any economies of scale) the components of growth in eleven countries are given in Table 4.

The importance of 'technical progress' *as calculated* stands out very clearly. Only in Netherlands 1954–9, Canada 1949–59, and Japan 1950–8 is the growth contribution of capital stock greater than that of technical progress. In most cases the technical progress contribution is considerably greater. However, before drawing any firm conclusions from these calculations it is important to consider the implications of the procedure adopted.

First, it is assumed that there are no economies of scale ($a + b = 1$). This is in line with Solow's finding for the United States ($a = 0·65$, $b = 0·35$) but not in line with the Gehrig and Kuhlo finding for West Germany ($a = 0·76$, $b = 0·34$). Because capital and labour tend to increase fairly steadily over time, multiple regression analysis finds it difficult to 'allocate' more-than-proportional increases in output as between increases in scale and the mere passage of time. In his study Solow pointed out that although the regressions seemed to favour the trend term this might simply be a consequence of its greater smoothness. The use of the Gehrig-Kuhlo values for a and b ($a + b > 1$ and $b > 0·3$) must bring down the value of z, though the fall is far from dramatic. For West Germany 1950–4, z falls from 5·6 to 5·4, and for 1954–9 from 3·5 to 3·2. In Japan 1950–8, z falls from 3·0 to 2·6. In the United Kingdom 1949–59, z falls from 1·2 to 1·0. In France and Italy 1949–59, z falls by 0·1.

TABLE 4

The Estimated Contribution to Growth of Gross Domestic Product (GDP)
of Increases of Labour Force, Capital Stock and 'Technical Progress'
in Selected Countries

Country and period	(%) Annual rates of growth of			(%) Estimated contribution to growth of		
	Labour	Capital	GDP	Labour	Capital	'Technical progress'
	1	*2*	*3*	*4*	*5*	*6*
Belgium						
1. 1949–54	0·6	2·4	3·6	0·4	0·7	2·5
2. 1954–9	− 0·1	2·7	2·3	− 0·1	0·8	1·6
Canada						
3. 1949–59	2·1	7·1	4·3	1·5	2·1	0·7
Netherlands						
4. 1949–54	1·4	4·0	4·9	1·0	1·2	2·7
5. 1954–9	1·1	5·5	4·1	0·8	1·7	1·6
Norway						
6. 1949–59	0·2	4·4	3·7	0·1	1·3	2·3
Sweden						
7. 1949–59	0·5	2·0	3·4	0·3	0·6	2·5
UK						
8. 1949–59	0·6	3·1	2·5	0·4	0·9	1·2
France						
9. 1949–54	0·1	2·9	4·8	0·1	0·9	3·8
10. 1954–9	0·2	3·9	4·1	0·1	1·2	2·8
Italy						
11. 1949–54	1·5	3·0	6·4	1·1	0·9	4·4
12. 1954–9	0·8	3·4	5·7	0·6	1·0	4·1
West Germany						
13. 1950–4	1·8	4·8	8·3	1·3	1·4	5·6
14. 1954–9	1·4	6·9	6·6	1·0	2·1	3·5
Israel						
15. 1952–8	3·3	11·8	9·8*	2·3	3·6	3·9
Japan						
16. 1950–8	2·4	10·6	7·9	1·7	3·2	3·0

* Net National Product.

Source: Aukrust, *Productivity Measurement Review*, February 1965.

Second, it is assumed that the rate of technical progress (z) is independent of the rate of growth of capital. On the face of it this is an unreal assumption. However, the statistics in Table 4 do not lend much support to a counter assumption that technical progress *must* enter the production function via the investment process and is therefore closely related to the growth rate of capital. The random relationship between the growth rates in capital and technical progress as computed is shown in Chart 2, where the numbers correspond to the entries in Table 4.

Third, a production function for the whole economy necessarily lumps together all forms of capital, although growth may be much more sensitive to some forms of investment than to others. This problem was considered in *Economic Survey of Europe 1961* when it was concluded that variations in incremental capital output ratios

Chart 2

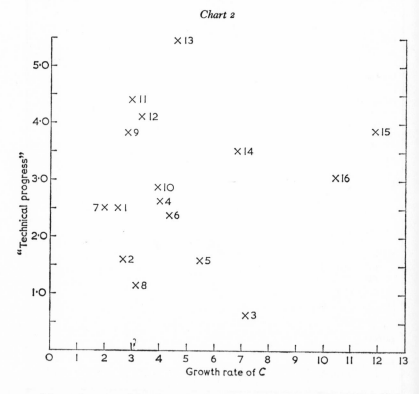

could not be traced back to the way in which investment had been distributed between different industries in different countries.

T. P. Hill[6] has tested the effect of separating out gross fixed investment into machinery, residential construction and other construction.

TABLE 5

Country	1954–62	1953–61			
		Average % share in GNP			
	Average annual % growth in real GNP per person employed	*Gross fixed investment*	*Gross fixed investment in*		
			Machinery and equipment	*Residential construction*	*Other construction*
France	4·74	18·3	8·3	4·5	5·5
Germany	4·50	22·5	11·6	5·2	5·7
Italy	4·33	20·8	9·0	5·4	6·4
USA	2·17	16·6	5·7	4·5	6·4
UK	1·87	15·2	7·8	3·1	4·3
Austria	4·92	21·1	11·1	4·1	5·9
Denmark	3·21	17·7	9·4	3·1	5·2
Netherlands	2·89	23·1	11·6	4·4	7·1
Sweden	2·77	20·9	7·4	5·2	8·3
Ireland	2·62	14·8	6·2	2·3	6·3
Belgium	2·39	17·2	7·7	5·2	4·3
Canada	2·01	23·8	8·1	4·7	11·0

The correlations given in Table 6 show that in so far as any general association exists between growth and investment in this period it was largely due to investment in machinery and equipment. For the

TABLE 6
Squared Correlation Coefficients

Type of investment	*Growth of GNP*	*Growth of GNP per person employed*
Share of gross fixed investment in GNP	0·49	0·11
Share of investment in machinery and equipment	0·49	0·36
Share of total construction	0·12	0·00
Share of residential construction	0·36	0·07
Share of other construction	0·01	0·05 (negative)

growth of GNP per person employed, all correlations, excepting machinery and equipment, were quite trivial.

Multiple regression analysis, with investment in machinery (M) and construction (C) as independent variables, and GNP per person employed (g) gave

$$g = 0.69 + 0.35M - 0.05C \quad (R^2 = 0.37)$$

Applying this equation to the data given in Table 5 gave the following relations between actual growth in GNP per head and the growth expected from the equation.[6]

TABLE 7

Annual Percentage Growth of Gross National Product

Country	Actual	'Expected' from equation	% Difference of 'expected' from actual
Germany	4·50	4·21	− 6·4
Italy	4·33	3·27	− 24·5
Austria	4·92	4·08	− 17·1
France	4·74	3·11	− 34·4
Denmark	3·21	3·56	+ 10·9
Netherlands	2·89	4·18	+ 44·6
Canada	2·01	2·78	+ 38·3
Sweden	2·77	2·64	− 4·7
USA	2·17	2·17	− 0·0
Belgium	2·39	2·92	+ 22·2
UK	1·87	3·05	+ 63·1
Ireland	2·62	2·42	− 6·5

The differences between actual and 'expected' rates of growth vary between 63·1% too high for the United Kingdom to 33·4% too low for France. The segregation of machinery and equipment from construction and the allowance for their differing effects on growth does insufficient to reinstate capital as the most important factor in economic growth.

It is therefore appropriate to consider further the residual factor, z, in economic growth. This residual catches factors in growth other than quantitative increases in L and C, and must therefore include such things as strength of pressures and opportunities in innovation, the structure of industry, the effects of investment in men as productive agents, the nature of Government economic policy, the community's interest in growth, and so on.

3. THE HUMAN FACTOR

Aukrust defined the human factor vaguely as 'organization, professional skills and technical knowledge'. He argued that we should pay more attention to man as a factor of production: 'We have tried to increase the rate of progress by keeping up the level of investment. We ought to reconsider our plans and policies and look into the possibilities of achieving greater gains by increasing our efforts in the fields of research and education.'[7]

There is now a considerable literature on the relation between research and growth. One of the early writers in this field was John Stuart Mill who was so excited by the possibilities of extending practical knowledge that he came near to suggesting that the growth in wealth had no limit.[8] Over one hundred years later R. H. Ewell in a much quoted paper[9] claimed a definite connection between growth rates of 3% in GNP and 10% in RandD and argued that if the growth rate in RandD should ever decline to 3% the economic growth rate would probably drop to $1-1\frac{1}{2}\%$ per year within five years.

The general idea that there is a causal relation between wealth and expenditure on RandD (generally expressed as a percentage of GNP: 'the RD rate') is very widespread. We are often assured that it is a source of economic weakness that our RD rate is less than the American.[10] There is also a widespread belief that we could achieve a very much higher rate of innovation in industry if RandD as a percentage of net output in 'backward industries' were raised to the level of that in 'progressive' industries. This appears to be what J. K. Galbraith is maintaining in his treatment of the economies of technical development in *American Capitalism* (1952).

That the main growth industries do have high RD rates is true (see Chapter VII); that the low-growth industries could become high-growth industries by raising their RD rates accordingly is almost certainly untrue. The high-growth industries have high RD rates because in these industries RandD is profitable. It is significant that the pattern of RD rates by industries is remarkably similar for advanced industrial countries. The growth potential of RandD varies enormously between industries.

RandD are needed to create new industries and sustain industrial growth in rich countries. Rich countries are also in a position to sustain a large higher education sector, and so to have a good supply of scientists and engineers. A rise in RandD (as a percentage of GNP) with output per head is therefore in general to be expected. Such a *general* rise is shown in Chart 3.

Chart 3

Research and Development Expenditure in Relation to Per Capita Gross National Product (at Market Prices) 1961 (or nearest year)

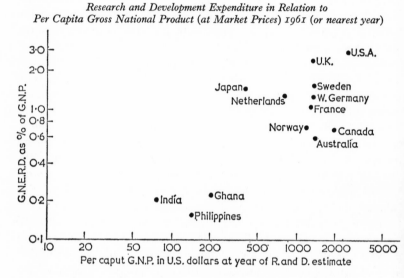

Source: *Science, Economic Growth, and Government Policy*, OECD, 1963.

It is clear from Chart 3 that there are very big differences in RD rates for the United Kingdom, Sweden, West Germany, and Australia although their levels of output per head are very similar. These differences become more significant when we consider growth, in which context we want to know the effect of RandD in stimulating growth. This is a difficult thing to measure. Time lags between RandD and innovation vary considerably, and RandD statistics are very fragmentary before 1950. However, such information as we have does not support the theory that there is a direct causal link between growth in output per head and the RandD percentage (see Chapter IV).

It would be easy to conclude from this that Aukrust's hopes for growth through research are misplaced. In fact, E. F. Dennison, by a different route, appears to arrive at just such a conclusion for the United States. Of the annual per *caput* measured growth rate of 1·7 from 1929–57, he estimates that only one-twelfth can be attributed to organized R and D.[11] His calculation is based in part on the observed failure of patents to rise despite the great increase in R and D expenditure, but mainly on the assumption that businessmen equate private rates of return on R and D and capital investment. However, even if *marginal* returns were the same on the two forms of expenditure, it does not follow that the *average* returns were not far apart but that the average returns from R and D were much higher. With the efficient rate of growth in R and D departments low,[12] short period marginal returns fall quite steeply. In so far as longer term yields to expansion are higher, we would expect a more rapid increase in the R and D share than in the investment share of GNP. This has in fact happened in both the United States and the United Kingdom where the R and D share has increased threefold in the last ten to twelve years.

It is not only the failure to distinguish between average and marginal returns that leads Dennison to a probable underestimate of the contribution of R and D. On the assumption that three-fifths of reported income differentials in incomes from work was due to differences in education, he estimates that 40% of growth per head was due to increased education. In this field the contributions of education and research are very difficult to separate. Without technological innovation (part of which was dependent on R and D of the period) the income differentials would presumably have been less.

However, the fact that Dennison has probably underestimated the contribution of R and D in United States growth does not dispose of the problem. Looked at internationally there is no sign that growth rates are increasing functions of RD rates. Nor do we find such a relation within countries. For thirty years R and D in the United States has been growing by 12% a year in real terms without any significant changes in the trend rates of growth of total output per head. The popular idea that R and D is the throttle of the economy and that if we want more speed (growth) we simply give the economy more throttle (raise the RD rate) has no foundation in fact.

This should not be surprising. The distinction between invention and innovation is well known. R and D is part of the invention process; innovation is another matter. Furthermore, most defence, medical, and university research, is not concerned with invention for growth. If we exclude defence R and D, the 'big three' (United Kingdom, United States, Russia) come close to the West German, French, and Japanese level for the period, but all this does is to reduce the suspicion of a perverse relationship between RD and growth rates.

Even Rand D concerned with new products and processes will not all lead to growth. Part of the Rand D will not yield inventions. Where it does, the inventions may be (i) unusable, (ii) usable but unused, (iii) used. Where the invention is used, i.e. becomes the basis of an innovation, it may have great or small growth potential, be taken up quickly or slowly, be managed well or poorly. For big yields to Rand D we need inventions with large-growth potential that are taken up quickly and well managed.

An invention will be economically worthless when the present value of prospective innovation based on it is zero or less. An invention will be usable but unused when there is a bad forecast of the commercial worth of an invention, or a shortage of risk capital or such a defect of industrial structure that it is not within the interest or capacity of any one firm to take up the invention, even though an industry with a different structure would. The literature on the economics of Rand D, the development gap, and the shortage of risk capital is concerned by implication with the problem of why we do not get a bigger yield from our Rand D expenditure (see Chapters IV and VI).

When an invention resulting from Rand D is used, the growth potential may be very great. This was the case with well-known new products such as nylon, terylene, transistors, polythene, silicones, and television, and new processes such as catalytic cracking, continuous casting, hot strip rolling, and float glass. But most usable Rand D output results in minor process or product improvement. Much process work, for example, is concerned with finding ways to offset rising wage or materials costs or to meet higher customer or competitor standards. Beyond a relatively low level, rising RD rates may not lead to anything like a proportionate rise in identifiable inventions, still less to those with considerable growth potential.[13]

When an invention has a considerable growth potential and is fully developed its yield will be higher if it is taken up quickly. But for a failure in structural design the quick commercial development of the Comet jet airliner would have paid off very handsomely. However, premature commercial development, which is often not possible to identify except after the event, is costly, as proved to be the case with the Comet and more recently with atomic power stations. Once a new product or process is proved the speed of its spread will have a very important effect on growth.

4. RESEARCH AND DEVELOPMENT AND THE
USE OF SCIENTISTS

The efficient choice of R and D projects, the speed of take-up of usable inventions, and efficiency in the management of innovation, depend in some measure on the deployment of scientific manpower. If scientists and engineers are not employed in production departments (and in some cases, in technical selling), R and D departments will not get sufficient information about the potential commercial significance of possible R and D projects and production departments will frequently be unable to judge the significance of R and D output or manage its application.[14] Because of this it is quite possible to have too much research; that is to say, too small a proportion of the scientific manpower in production, selling, and (also) administration, to squeeze the maximum growth potential out of scientific and technical knowledge. It is a great mistake to treat technology and current R and D as synonymous. They are not.

The importance of distinguishing between technology and one's current R and D becomes greater when we take into account the international nature of, and international trade in, knowledge and knowhow. The idea that in each country there is a closed flow system in which innovation follows from invention or development which follows from applied research, which follows from basic research, is quite wrong. It is perfectly possible to innovate without any R and D expenditure of one's own at all, by relying on the R and D of other countries and the inventiveness of scientists and engineers in production. It is also perfectly possible to ignore basic research, even applied research, and to conduct successful development.

All countries borrow or buy knowhow from other countries, in the form of purchasing journals, attending conferences, buying knowhow, or allowing overseas companies to operate. Some countries rely more than others on international exchange in this field. The smaller the scientific manpower base, the more will it be economic to stress development rather than research and to buy knowhow abroad. Australia is a conspicuous example of a very small dependent economy in this respect. France, Germany, and Japan also draw in much more knowledge and knowhow than they give out. By contrast the United States receives six times more in fees and royalties than it pays out (see Chapter I).

The implication of my argument is fairly plain, namely, that

international exchange of technical knowledge is beneficial, just as
international exchange of goods is beneficial. Attempted self-
sufficiency in either field retards growth, particularly in small
countries. Failure to take this and the dependence of innovation on
the employment of scientists and engineers outside R and D into
account, has led, at any rate in the United Kingdom, to a seriously
misplaced pride in high R D rates. It is foolish to consider R D rates
without reference to the scientific manpower base.

5. TECHNICAL PROGRESS AND INVESTMENT

I now return to the question of whether expenditure on R and D and
education and on investment act independently on growth. In many
cases the expenditure on R and D and education leading to technical
progress will have to be embodied in the appropriate capital goods
before it can have an effect on output. This is obvious in the cases of:
(i) new industries made possible by technical progress; and (ii) new
machines (neutral or labour saving) so productive as to force the
obsolescence of existing machines.

There will be other cases where no investment is involved at all.
Many advances in technical or managerial knowledge simply lead to
better industrial housekeeping. This happens where for given hours
of work and prices, value of output per unit capital is increased. The
reduction of loss, which may be due, for example, to analysis and
control of raw materials or of temperature or pressure in processing,
will improve the output-capital ratio. So too will an increase in the
rate of throughput which may follow research into optimum temperatures and pressures.[15] Better design which improves quality and
value of output will have the same effect.

The less obvious cases arise where technical progress is embodied
in new equipment but is covered in the gross but not the net investment process.[16] Where there is technical progress some growth will
automatically flow from the replacement process. For example,
when the Austin Motor Company first installed automatic transfer
machines it found that the cost of these machines was less than the
cost (new) of the individual machine tools due to be replaced. There
are also very substantial capital-saving inventions in many new
fields. Thus in atomic energy, re-design of power stations has made
possible a 50% reduction in capital cost per unit output.

Will improvements in the output-capital ratios simply raise
investment via a rise in the profit rate? If so, better housekeeping and

capital-saving inventions would (with a time lag) simply increase investment and we would appear to be back in the world where the rate of growth depended directly on the capital stock. Even though some technical progress occurred without investment it would appear from the crude statistics not to do so.

Improvements in the capital-output ratio (valued at constant prices) in particular firms need not raise the rate of profit. Whether it does so or not will depend on competitive pressure in the industry. If the increased efficiency is passed on in the form of lower prices (or as is frequently the case, is made to restore profit margins) the rate of profit will not rise. From the standpoint of the firm the capital-output ratio will not fall; from the standpoint of measurement of capital stock and GNP in constant prices it will. It follows that only part of the improvements in capital-output ratios would be obscured by consequential changes in investment.

6. SCIENCE AND FORMS OF GROWTH

So far the possible contributions of technical progress (the human factor) to economic growth has been dealt with in a very general way. To take the matter further we need to distinguish between growth in product, growth in product per head, and growth in product per man-hour. These measures of growth may move in quite different ways.

Perhaps the biggest impact of the human factor has been to offset diminishing returns. The continuing revolution in the production of food has made possible a growth in output and population which was inconceivable even fifty years ago. Human ingenuity has also made possible the substitution of new materials for depleted natural resources. In both cases science makes possible growth in GNP as such without any *necessary* growth in the other measures.

The human factor is also responsible for creating new investment outlets. In the absence of these new outlets growth in GNP per head would tail off. The more mature a country, the less it can take over the more advanced technology of other countries, the more it needs new invention to stop a fall in the rate of growth in output per head. It is for this reason that it is possible for people like Ewell to count the share of science based new processes and products in current production, and from it to deduce R and D contributions to growth rates which apparently do not square with the evidence in Chart 1 in Chapter IV. In countries like the United States a great deal of invention (and therefore R and D) is required to prevent a fall in growth per head.

The impact of medical science on the expectation of life has produced a big effect on the age distribution of the population. Where the proportion of population at work is falling, growth in product per head and in product per man employed need not move together. Product per man employed could rise while product per head remained constant or even fell. An additional contribution from the human factor is therefore sometimes required to offset another tendency to reduce growth in product per head.

Product per man-hour could also rise when product per head and product per man did not. Suppose that there were no product innovations, and that all process innovations simply saved labour. In this case the effect of the human factor would be to reduce the working week (or the proportion at work) and to raise product per man-hour. Now a great deal of the impact of the human factor, and in particular of innovations in management methods is of this form. The tendency of product per man-hour to rise is often checked by product innovations because either there is a product 'improvement' which is not reflected in statistics of G N P, or the product per man-hour is relatively low in new forms of production in the early stages. In the latter case the product per man-hour will later rise, at least in the case of successful innovations.

Very many attempts to calculate the growth contributions of the human factor in general and of R and D in particular have been misleading because of a failure to specify either the precise measure of growth in mind or the relevance of that growth measure. In this field we have given insufficient thought to plausible models of growth in its various forms.

REFERENCES

1. GUSTAV CASSEL, *The Nature and Necessity of Interest* (Macmillan, 1903) and *The Theory of Social Economy* (Benn, 1932).
2. O. AUKRUST, *Productivity Measurement Review* (February 1959).
3. O. AUKRUST and J. BJERKE, 'Real Capital and Economic Growth in Norway 1900–56', *Income and Wealth*, Series VIII (London, 1959).

4. R. SOLOW, 'Technical Change and the Aggregate Production Function', *Review of Economics and Statistics* (August 1957).

5. G. GEHRIG and K. C. KUHLO, *I.F.O. Studien, 7 Jahrgang* Parts 1 and 2 (1961).

6. T. P. HILL, 'Growth and Investment According to International Comparisons', *Economic Journal* (June 1964).

7. O. AUKRUST, op. cit.

8. J. S. MILL, *Principles of Political Economy*, Book 4, Chapter 1, Section 2 (1848).

9. R. H. EWELL, *Chemical and Engineering News* (1955), pp. 2,980–6.

10. A. SHONFIELD once argued that, because it is the absolute level of RandD expenditure that matters, we cannot hope to compete with advancing United States technology over a wide range of industry without spending at least two or three times as much as we do at present (*Encounter*, September 1959). That is to say *all* our scientists and engineers should be engaged in RandD. If innovation really did depend on one's own RandD the outlook for the small countries would be very grim indeed. In fact it does not. I examined this problem for Australia in *Industrial Research and Economic Growth* (1962), Chapter VIII of this book.

11. E. F. DENNISON, *Sources of Economic Growth in the United States* (CED, 1962), Chapter 21. He places the contribution of RandD to true growth higher. True growth is greater than measured growth because 'the introduction of new or better final products, and of cheaper final products if they differ in physical characteristics from the old, does not in general increase the measured national product'.

12. C. F. CARTER and B. R. WILLIAMS, *Industry and Technical Progress* (Oxford University Press, 1957), Chapter 6. This is partly a matter of the rate at which production departments can absorb new knowledge, and partly of the elasticity of supply of scientists. With low elasticities of supply, the time required to absorb newcomers, and possibly the need to recruit less-able scientists, research managers would expect rising marginal costs and falling marginal yields from expansion, despite very high average yields in relation to average costs.

13. DENNISON, op. cit., p. 233. According to F. A. Howard, 'the United States output of inventions per head is not only low in the list of industrial countries but has declined much more over the

last thirty years than that of other leading industrial nations'. (Address to Patent, Trademark and Copyright Foundation). Even though patent statistics are defective as measures of inventions, they do provide some guide.

14. These points are developed at length in C. F. CARTER and B. R. WILLIAMS, *Science in Industry* (Oxford University Press, 1959).

15. For examples see B. R. WILLIAMS, 'Notes on Cost and Capacity', *The Manchester School* (September 1961).

16. W. E. G. SALTER, *Productivity and Technical Change* (Cambridge University Press, 1960).

X

Information and Criteria
in Capital Expenditure Decisions*

Research into capital expenditure decisions in industry is concerned first of all with establishing and comprehending the facts. This article summarizes the results of studies carried out from the Centre for Business Research in the University of Manchester, and attempts to interpret them. Once the facts have been understood, the policy implications can be drawn out, whether for Governments concerned with national employment and growth policy, or for individual firms (or 'business schools') concerned with improving decisions.

Much of the early research grew directly from the traditional theory of the firm. In that theory, firms are assumed to maximize profits, not because they have no other interests but from the pressure of competition. Now a necessary though a far from sufficient condition of maximum profits is that capital projects with prospective rates of return less than the rate of interest should not be undertaken, and that all projects with prospective rates of return greater than the rate on borrowed money should be.

In calculating rates of return, allowance should be made for discounting. This we can do by using either the 'internal rate of return' or the 'present value' method. With the internal rate of return method, estimated cash inflows and cash outflows over the life of the project are discounted at a rate that will equalize them over the life of the project. When this rate is greater than the rate on borrowed money, the project will add to profits and vice versa. With the second method, future net cash flows are discounted to give a present value for the project. Where this is positive, the project will add to profits and vice versa.

Inquiries into what firms actually do have shown that the traditional theory of the firm is not a simple mirror of business behaviour even in competitive conditions. For many projects prospective yields are not calculated. Where they are, the calculations are often extremely

*First appeared in *The Journal of Management Studies*, September 1964.

crude. For example, it is quite usual to calculate the rate of return from estimates of yield in a 'representative year' or simply from the 'first year of full working'. In judging projects, firms able to borrow at similar rates sometimes set very different cut-off rates of return. Other firms do not use cut-off or pass rates of return at all, but judge a project from the period of payback. Still other firms that make calculations of prospective rates of return appear to regard these calculations as unimportant by comparison with qualitative factors. The proportion of firms that use either the internal rate of return or the present value methods expounded in the traditional theory of the firm appears to be very small indeed.

I. THE PRACTICE OF THIRTEEN FIRMS

At the Centre for Business Research we have recently completed a general study of investment procedures in thirteen of our member firms and a detailed study of a substantial investment project in each firm.* From these substantial investment projects (which in fact provide a fairly good guide to general investment behaviour in these firms) we found the following.

In four cases, calculations of yield were not made at all. In Case 1, involving a royalty as a percentage of sales value, with a specified minimum, an estimate was made of the sales volume for the new product required to meet the specified minimum. Without the aid of a quantitative market evaluation, more than this sales volume was assumed to be attainable. The firm was mistaken. In Case 2, although the firm had a formal procedure for calculation of yield prior to investment decisions it was not followed in this case. Although this was not a quick decision forced by outside pressure, the evaluation related purely to the technological problems of the new product. Case 3 was concerned only with an improved process. The calculation was purely technological. In fact the financial yield which we were able to calculate was enormous and, according to the traditional theory of the firm, should have induced action years earlier. In Case 4, involving the use of a computer for data processing, attention was concentrated on the feasibility and then the reliability of the operation. It was simply taken for granted that if automatic data processing plant could be used and was reliable it should be used.

---

* The field work was conducted by W. P. Scott, assisted by J. S. Smith and C. B. Troughton. In the preparation of this paper I had long discussions with Mr Scott on the interpretation of the case material. No difference in meaning is intended between the word 'investment' and the phrase 'capital expenditure'.

In the nine cases where yield calculations were made, the firms had an established cut-off rate of return. Yet in four of the cases (5–8) accepted projects had rates of return *below*, or possibly below, the cut-off rate.

In Case 5, expected pretax yield was only 10% for the first seven years. Thereafter yield was expected to improve but by how much was not calculated. Nevertheless, there were said to be important qualitative factors in favour, and the project was judged to be in the interests of the long-term growth of the company. In Case 6 (which, like 5, involved a new factory), yield was calculated as between 10% (at 80% capacity and a conservative estimate of prices) and 22% (at full capacity and favourable prices). With a cut-off yield of 15% this was a doubtful project which was nevertheless agreed. Then before construction was started the director in charge changed the scale and form of the investment to make it 'less of a gamble'. In Case 7 an investment with a prospective yield of 7–10% was accepted, despite an agreed cut-off level of 15%, on the grounds that there would be substantial intangible benefits in addition. In Case 8 the prospective yield from a computer installation was calculated by consultants as in the range of 5–20%. With a cut-off level of 15% this was on quantitative grounds a very doubtful project. Yet the firm was less impressed by the quantitative estimates than by the possibility of a computer 'helping us to run the business better', a matter on which the consultants' claims had been extremely vague.

In two of the remaining five cases (9 and 10), pretax prospective yields were calculated as 24–44% and 15%, in both cases above the cut-off level. In Case 11 a discounted cash flow approach was used. The calculated internal rate of return was well above the rate of interest. In Cases 12 and 13, mergers, the problem was one of estimating a capital value. In Case 12, a discounted cash flow approach was used and calculations of the present value of assets guided the calculations. In Case 13 the stock exchange valuation was used as the basis.

2. POSSIBLE REASONS FOR THE RELATIONSHIP BETWEEN CRITERIA AND DECISIONS

How should such behaviour be interpreted? As a sign that competitive pressure is so weak as to leave ample room for non-profit goals? As a sign that most decision-takers are rather muddled and should be packed off to a good business school? As a sign that the factors in investment decisions are often too complex to be summarized in yield calculations, whether discounted or not?

(*a*) *That competitive pressure is so weak as to leave ample room for non-profit goals.* The assumption of profit maximization does not imply a judgement that the basic motive for business actions is profit-making, simply that in a competitive economy it is a condition of survival. The weaker the competitive pressure the greater the room for other motives. Can we explain the behaviour of firms that did not even calculate prospective yields (1–4) and of those that calculated yields but ignored their standard cut-off rates (5–8) in terms of weak competition?

It is, of course, difficult to measure competitive pressure. To say that competition in an industry is strong because the number of firms is large and restrictive practices few, and vice versa, is quite misleading. Pressure to make the most profitable use of resources may be much stronger in few-firm than in many-firm industries. This will indeed be so where rapid innovation is part of competitive process in the former but not in the latter.

Of Cases 1–4 I would argue that in three of the firms the market pressure to make profitable use of resources was strong. Of Cases 5–8 the market pressure was also strong in three cases. It is not possible to make any clear distinction between Cases 1–4, 5–8, and 9–13 in terms of competitive situations.

It would not be appropriate to speculate about the general strength (or weakness) of competitive pressure in United Kingdom industry, though it is relevant to consider the suggestion that competitive pressure to maximize profits must be weak because firms just don't attempt it. Do these case studies throw any direct light on that argument, sometimes found in the form that 'profit maximization went out with the managerial revolution'?

It is not possible here to give an account of the complex responses to our questions about the objectives of investment projects. Such responses need to be interpreted with very great care. In a particular investment there may have been half a dozen key people all of whom had different things in mind. It is easy to draw quite the wrong conclusion by failing to distinguish between the spur to, or interest in, some activity, and the potential effect on profits. The person who sponsors some proposal to invest in innovation may be concerned only with technical (or even personal) achievement, but his proposal may be finally accepted because of its calculated or assumed effect on profits (or on such things as stability, growth, or market share).

It is often assumed that the use of criteria such as stability, growth, or market share demonstrate the importance of non-profit goals. They may, but they may not. In an uncertain world, calculations about the effects of investment must be speculative, at times very speculative, and in such conditions relating investment projects to their probable effects on turnover or market share may be thought of as reasonable 'rule of thumb' procedures for achieving satisfactory returns to capital employed.

Now if it is said that this shifts the attention from maximizing to what Simon calls 'satisficing' behaviour I would not disagree. In any case it does not much matter here. For the very concept of maximizing behaviour is only clear cut when there is little uncertainty and we do not have to worry about possible conflicts between short-period and long-period maximization. I return to these points below.[1]

(b) That decision-makers rely on faulty methods of appraisal. Another possible explanation of the behaviour in Cases 1–8 is that the firms concerned are just plain inefficient. Most academic economists would probably conclude from the evidence of investment case studies that there were clear signs of intellectual muddle and inefficiency. In this they would certainly be joined by a good many management consultants and industrial economists.[2]

It is easy to build up a formidable criticism of the methods used by most of the firms. The first criticism relates to the method of estimating prospective yields. Usually big assumptions have to be made not only about the costs of using an untried method and about market growth, but also about competitors' reactions. In some of the cases mentioned in Section I pessimistic and optimistic estimates of prospective yield were made. Thus in Case 6 the yield was calculated as 10–22%; in Case 7, 7–12%, in Case 8, 5–20%; in Case 9, 24–44%. In other cases the range of possible movement was not calculated because either one outcome only was considered, or a 'reasonably safe outcome' was chosen. Yet to us, doubtless with the advantage of hindsight, the crucial assumption about the future had frequently been made early in the calculations, buried in the estimates and never critically examined. In these conditions we were not surprised by large divergencies between forecast and achieved yields. Thus in Case 9 where forecast yields were in the range 24–44%, achieved yield was under 10%. In Case 7 where forecast yield was 7–12%, substantial losses were made.

Nor, except in one case, did we find attention given to the range of possible gains and losses. Yet the latter calculation, involving an estimate of the capital at risk, must be of significance.

The usual cut-off or pass rates of return can also be made to look rather disreputable. Take the common habit of using a cut-off rate of 15% average undiscounted yield pre-tax. Three strong logical objections can be made. First, the calculation is very sensitive to the depreciation period, which may be determined by Inland Revenue practices and not by the probable life of the plant. Second, it ignores the powerful effects of investment allowances on cash flows. Third, it cannot distinguish between projects with the same average returns but different patterns of profit over time.

Mr Alfred[2] has shown just how misleading the traditional business criterion of something like 15% yield (after depreciation but before tax) can be. 15% on a type of project where earnings build up slowly may give a discounted cash flow (DCF) return in the region of 10%. Yet a 10% DCF return on a plant improvement where the earnings begin immediately might imply only an 8% traditional return. By contrast a 10% DCF return on the acquisition of an existing business might require something like 20% traditional return.

Clearly this is a powerful line of criticism. The use of DCF techniques would bring very large changes in the investment policies of many firms. This would be so not only because of its effects on the apparent profitability of various types of projects, but also because of its effect in forcing a quite different view of the cost of capital.

Yet this is by no means the end of the matter. Although economists are not likely to criticize the logic of the DCF approach – it is essentially 'the economists' ' method – the application of the method is far from straightforward. How far can the likely outcome of an investment be summarized as a prospective yield? If the numerical estimates are subject to very wide margins of error is it possible that sophisticated techniques will cause over-attention to the problem of evaluation, and so cause neglect of the very shaky statistical foundations of the whole enterprise?

(c) *That the factors involved are too complex to be summarized numerically.* We come then to the third possible explanation – that the factors involved in an investment decision are too complex to be summarized numerically. All the firms in our sample distinguished between quantitative and qualitative considerations, that is to say, between numerical and non-numerical implications. Most of them also distinguished between documented and non-documented information.

These distinctions make it plain that the yield calculations mentioned in Section 1 were not treated as a complete guide to the profit implications of the investment decisions. But why were these numerical implications not expressed even though they could only be expressed within a fairly wide range? To explain that, it is necessary to distinguish between the nature of information and the attitude to that information, and between the range of factors included in the documented case presented for decision, and the range of factors taken into account by those making the decision.

Calculations of prospective yield from an investment project must be based on forecasts of fixed and working capital, costs per unit output, and value of sales. Each forecast will be subject to a margin of error. With a new process, the estimate of fixed capital may not be a good guide to subsequent tender prices. (In Case 9, for example, the capital costs were 25% above estimates.) The estimates of cost per unit output will be based on not only forecasts of capital costs and the costs of material inputs, but also of the efficiency of management. Forecasts of the latter must be 'up in the air' until the management team and their attitudes to the project are known. Forecasts of sales depend on a forecast of market growth and a forecast of market share which in turn depends on a forecast of competitors' plans and responses. The greater the departure from familiar territory the greater the difficulty of forecasting.

The novelty involved may be in technology or in marketing. In Case 6 involving both a process new to the firm and a product well outside their traditional markets, the most serious error of forecast was of demand. Unexpectedly enough, their error was not in the forecast of market growth but in the estimate of the current demand. They calculated that it was twice as great as it subsequently proved to be.

Given these uncertainties it is possible to end up with a tremendous gap between optimistic and pessimistic forecasts of yield. The cases we quoted of 5–20%, 20–40%, and 10–22% could very easily have been wider. Indeed the lower limits on both the 20–40% and the 5–20% forecasts were proved by events to be ten percentage points too high. The point that this divergence between forecast and event induced the firms to take remedial action will be taken up in Section 4.

The estimates of yield are often, we have seen, incomplete. Thus it may be thought that a proposed investment project would give the firm valuable experience of a new technology. This experience might be thought very valuable in preparing entry to a product field with a high growth potential or in preparing the way for later changes in processes. Yet the firm may be quite unprepared to put a monetary value on this experience and prefer to treat it as a favourable qualitative factor. Another project might be thought likely to lead to research on development projects of a kind that would attract very able scientists and engineers (or make it possible to retain or attract first rate managers) and so add to the long term growth potential of the firm. Another might be thought hazardous to goodwill because it involved 'competing with good customers', or because it involved entry to a field of, say, 'one-armed bandits' which would tarnish the firm's public image.

Given the number of factors involved and the potential errors of forecast in each case, the forecast yield must be subject to very wide margins of error. It is therefore not altogether surprising that many firms refuse to guess the numerical implications of more qualitative factors. These qualitative factors may, however, play an important part in two ways. They may be used, first, to add (or subtract) an undefined number of percentage points to a yield calculation. Thus in Case 5, for example, with a forecast yield of 10%, the judgement that the project would, *inter alia*, greatly increase the chance of getting into a connected set of growth fields was used to bolster the numerical estimates. The firm was not prepared to say that the numerical implication of qualitative factors was $x\%$ but it was prepared to go ahead *as if* a complete numerical estimate would have shown a numerical yield of not 10% but (at least) 15%. Qualitative estimates may also be used to increase (or reduce) confidence in the yield calculations. Thus in Case 6 the qualitative factors engendered a feeling of confidence that the most likely yield was well above the lower limit of 10%. When, after the decision to proceed, more detailed engineers' estimates were received, this confidence was shaken and both the scale and form of the project were changed.

The importance of the distinction between documented and non-documented factors depends on the way in which the project originates and on the way in which the calculations are made. A manager with a very good profit record may present his case in terms of turnover or market share and make no calculation of prospective yield on the capital involved. In such a case those making the decision may simply assume that the manager uses rule of thumb methods which produce the profits, or do some 'back of the envelope figuring' about the likely effects on profits of a change in turnover or market share produced at the capital cost proposed. Cases 2 and 3 can be explained partly in these terms. Projects of this kind are unlikely to be far away from familiar territory.

With a project originating from the board, the policy implications or the qualitative factors considered important by the board may be put on paper. If, however, the project originates lower down, what the final decision takers regard as the important policy or qualitative implications of the proposals may never appear on paper. A project which appears on paper with a high prospective yield may be rejected because of its assumed bad effect on goodwill – a factor which the documented case may have ignored. Alternatively the board may prefer a project with a relatively low yield to one with a higher yield because it is more consistent with a line of policy on which it has decided but which it has not announced. Once again, the numerical implications may never be made explicit though the board may have decided on this line of policy (maybe diversification) to improve or maintain the earning capacity of the firm.

Policy decisions of this kind may well involve preparation now for events in a rather indeterminate future. In this they are similar to many research projects. If with such projects we use the 'internal rate of return' variant of DCF methods, the projects may be made to look weak in relation to projects with a short-term but not long-term profit potential. This tendency would be reinforced whenever firms were not prepared to put numbers to favourable qualitative considerations. Faced with the results of such a method of evaluation businessmen might react strongly against DCF methods. There is a problem of substance here. There is no logical reason why the same discount rate should be used for all projects. Given the duty of directors to consider the earning capacity of the firm over time, it would be wrong to use a discounting method which cut out projects, including research projects, likely to be needed to maintain future profits. The choice of projects with highest internal rates of return could however have this effect. However, if the present value method is used, discount rates appropriate to different projects could be explicitly considered and chosen.

3. ORIGINS, RECOGNITION AND INVESTIGATION OF INVESTMENT PROJECTS

So far, nothing has been said about the origins of investment projects,

K

and little about the processes of investigation which are far from costless and presumably, therefore, are economized in some way or other.

One of the outstanding impressions from our study of investment procedures was the absence of competition between projects. The number of projects carefully considered but rejected appeared to be small. We were often reminded of the Sherlock Holmes case concerning the dog that did not bark. The creation or recognition of investment opportunities by firms is a matter calling for more extensive investigation.

For profitable investment decisions (other than simple replacement) there must be an opportunity given by such things as market growth, new or improved products, cost reducing innovations, or mergers.

The simplest cases of recognizing 'opportunities' may follow from direct pressure such as breakdown in plant or equipment. There may also be proposals from outsiders. These may be offers for licensing arrangements, proposals for joint investments, requests from important customers (including Government) for special products or additional products implying additional capacity, or 'feelers' for mergers or takeovers.

More difficult cases arise from indirect pressures to find or create opportunities, perhaps simply to find ways of keeping in a competitive race over time. Relieving excessive competitive pressure on profit margins or output may require process or product innovations or both. Such innovation may be deliberately created by R and D within the firm. However, not all opportunities for innovation are new. The firm may by improvements in internal management or marketing place itself in a position to make profitable use of processes or products previously ignored.

The process of recognition may be much more complex. Two of our cases provide examples. In one case a firm making intermediate products for sale to industrial customers started a small testing section which assembled the products; then over the course of the years it came to sell the assembled products and so, without any formal decision to compete with customers, developed an additional activity. When the implication of this casual development was recognized by top management a formal decision was made to develop the new product line. The board of another firm, wishing to consolidate an existing market, agreed to purchase a new subsidiary. Members of middle management in the organization, who had been quietly canvassing the need for a policy of diversification into a broader product range, recognized that such a takeover would bring in a subsidiary which would both consolidate existing activities and lead into a broader range. It 'sold' the proposal to the board of the firm as a consolidation measure.

In the majority of cases we studied, the opportunity did not emerge suddenly, but had been 'in the back of people's minds' for some time. Influences leading to a more conscious recognition of opportunity have included growing evidence that the firm was not fully exploiting its potential share of a market, leading to a proposal to expand capacity or product range; evidence that other firms had already acted or were considering action (e.g. to instal computers); apparently chance factors – such as casual conversation or browsing through literature – which precipitated recognition or a judgement that an effort to promote the idea would be worthwhile.

The ability to recognize and to profit from technical innovations and market changes is related to a firm's activities and attitudes. Each firm has plant and equipment adapted to its existing products, a manufacturing and marketing knowhow, a reputation with customers, and relationships with suppliers and competitors. Many changes in markets and technologies may be noticed but ruled out as irrelevant to these activities and relations.

However, often the issue will not be so simple. The firm may have the technical and marketing knowhow (or be able to acquire it easily), but decide that there is not a profitable opportunity for them to use it. This may be because such an investment decision would force them into competition with established suppliers or customers and lead to a loss of established business; or into a possibly unsound degree of diversification.

Clearly, capacities to derive profit from a particular change in markets and technology must vary enormously between firms. But not all decisions will be either easy to make or, when made, sensible to the external observer. A firm may not notice, or it may refuse to consider seriously, an opportunity simply because 'it is not our line of business', or because it would 'disturb the balance' of the firm. As an example of the first, a shipbuilder might refuse opportunities to make houses or one-armed bandits because they are 'shipbuilders and proud of it'. The second may be of great importance in firms with well established product divisions. There the managers of, say, the heavy products division may have much greater power and prestige than the managers of light products, and be opposed to investment decisions that might undermine their power. Such managerial *attitudes* must play a part in determining the effective supply of investment opportunities.

For investment opportunities that are considered, I may have seemed to imply that there are three serial processes involved – first investigation or collection of the evidence, then evaluation of the evidence, then a decision. In fact, investigation and evaluation are very often not preliminaries to a decision but fused with it.

Although sometimes the cost (in men and money) of investigation and evaluation is small (the position with many problems of replacement) frequently the cost is considerable. This is the position, for example, with supersonic airliners or atomic power stations. But even the investigation of computers for commercial data processing may be quite expensive. In one case we examined, 1,000 men-days were put into the build up of information in addition to consultants' fees of the order of £10,000. Costly investigations are often based on something like an agreement in principle from the beginning, and then, for a decision not to proceed, the facts as they emerge may have to be very much against the project.

This likelihood of a gradual commitment to a project before investigation and evaluation is complete may be specially great when 'policy issues' are involved. Questions about such things as the balance of production, desirable growth rates, relations with competitors and suppliers, may have to be answered before agreement to commit resources to investigation and evaluation. This may create groupings and attitudes within the top management which almost predetermine the decision.

But even in the absence of an early decision in principle, it is important to emphasize the difference between the investment decision and the first recognition of a possible investment opportunity. Between the decision and the recognition there may be months of expensive investigation and evaluation. Many investment decisions will therefore depend on (i) the recognition of a possibility on the basis of very little evidence, perhaps on a hunch; and (ii) sufficient confidence of the outcome to commit management and financial resources to an investigation and evaluation of the project. If the person who proposes is not in the position to commit the company then he must be sufficiently persuasive (and perhaps skilful in selecting the person or persons to be persuaded) to induce those with that power to take the decision to investigate.

In the major cases studied in which the originator has not been a director, a particularly important step has been the acquisition of a director as patron before the proposal was formalized.

The nature of this rather mixed up process of investigation, evaluation and decision points the need for rather more thought about two issues. The first is the importance of certain crucial assumptions used both in the numerical forecasts and in the weight appropriate to qualitative factors. In our case studies we were surprised by the lack of critical attention given to the identification and assessment of the crucial assumptions, which may be far more important than the arithmetic of the operation. But if on the quantitative side the role of the arithmetic is sometimes over-stressed, on the qualitative side the arithmetic is usually under-stressed. Putting rough numbers to the possible profit significance of qualitative factors – 'it might add up to two percentage points but not six'; 'it might, together with these other factors add between one and five percentage points'; 'the chance that this would be significant is one in three'; and so on – is an effective way of concentrating thought about their significance.

The second issue requiring more thought is that of the process which throws up investment projects for consideration. In firms with R and D departments there is an important group with a professional interest in creating investment projects. However, their interest is necessarily limited, and it may be that even in such firms more formal provision should be made for a systematic search for preliminary evaluation of investment possibilities.

4. MAKING FORECASTS COME TRUE

The critical test of any investment project can only come after it has been taken. This is the element of truth in the assertion that was made to us on several occasions that 'the important thing in business is not to make good forecasts but to make them come true'.

An essentially sound investment may be made to appear weak by a poor management of the project. Conversely a poor investment scheme may be made to appear sound by brilliant management. When it is said that a firm pays less attention to the documented case for any investment project than to the man or men involved, it is this aspect of the investment project that is being stressed. This stress on importance of managing the investment also explains the emphasis some firms give to getting the agreement of the interested parties.

Given the crucial importance of successful operation and the chance that those opposed to or sceptical about the project might not work very hard to overcome difficulties, to base a decision solely on the basis of a paper case made without reference to personalities could be misguided.

Some idea of the significance of this comes obliquely from examples of remedial action taken when post-decision events confounded forecasts. In Case 9, where forecast yield was 24–44%, the yield achieved after two years of operation was only 9%. The capital cost had been 25% greater and the product prices lower than forecast. Yet after a re-appraisal of the project it was found that by a small increase in capital expenditure plant capacity could be increased by 50%. This formed the essential basis of remedial action, and the yield was moved into the forecast range. In Case 7, where forecast yield was 7–12%, a loss estimated at £500,000 concentrated management attention on the problem. After technical and managerial changes the loss was stopped and yield raised, though not yet into the forecast range. In Case 2, where a yield was not calculated, sales fell well below prediction. Management responsibilities and procedures were changed and sales were quickly raised to forecast levels.

In these cases there was a specific expectation of performance against which events could be judged. When there was a serious failure of performance action was taken. In certain cases performance was brought up to forecast despite excess capital cost or unfavourable price movement. There was 'slack' in the production system that could be taken up.

There is no reason to suppose that this slack would have been exploited if the initial results had been thought satisfactory. Equally, there is no clear evidence that projects in which there was no corrective action did not have some slack in them. If this slack exists for all investments, or even for a majority, the implications are far reaching.

When we discussed the problems with our firms we found a general agreement that there is a normal slack. As some put it: 'you can always find 10% economy somewhere if you look hard enough. This is what management consultants live on'.

This has implications for procedures which might improve investment performance. Management has many jobs to do. A crisis area draws management attention. When the outcome of an investment is notably below expectation, a special effort is made to improve performance. Yet a project which is running according to plan might show a much higher yield to special management attention.

REFERENCES

1. See also C. F. CARTER and B. R. WILLIAMS, *Investment in Innovation*, Chapters 3 and 4 (Oxford University Press, 1958).
2. See, for example, A. S. ASHTON, 'Investment Planning by Private Enterprise', *Lloyds Bank Review* (October 1962); and A. M. ALFRED, 'Discounted Cash Flow: The Proper Assessment of Investment Projects', *Investment Analyst* (December 1963).

XI

Planning and Technical Progress in Russia*

Rapid technical progress is a very important objective of the Russian social system. It is seen both as a condition of growth in output, and as a justification of the claim that a Communist régime, freed from 'the contradictions of the capitalist system', can manage the advanced forces of production made possible by modern science and technology more efficiently than any other system.

By comparison with the United States and the United Kingdom, Russia uses a low proportion of its scientists and engineers in R and D activities. There are three reasons for this. The first is that they have a uniform technological policy which reduces the amount of competitive R and D. The second is that they do not waste much effort in re-inventing: they have well organized arrangements for gathering in scientific and technical information from other countries; they buy machines, machine tools and scientific instruments from other countries, and both copy and adapt them for their own production; they make contracts with the West for complete plant and knowhow both in new fields of production and in fields where they have lagged behind. The third reason is that Russia has placed very great emphasis on 'investment in man' and they now have a very good supply of scientific manpower.

I. SCIENTIFIC MANPOWER AND RESEARCH

In Russia the term 'scientist' includes social scientists and humanists. Davies, Barker, and Fakiolas, in the OECD publication *The Research and Development Effort*, have estimated that after making allowance for this the total number of employed qualified scientists and engineers as defined in the United Kingdom was 2,780,000 in 1960 and 3,176,000 in 1962. If this is the correct figure, the Russian scientific manpower position is substantially better than the

* Written after a visit to Russia with the Minister of Technology in May 1966.

American. Davies, Barker, and Fakiolas also calculated that the number of qualified scientists and engineers engaged on RandD in 1962 was (the full time equivalent of) 487,000 if half the scientists and engineers employed by the project-design organizations are treated as engaged on RandD, or 416,000 if project and design organizations are assumed not to be involved in genuine RandD. If we take the higher figure of 487,000 (compared to the United States figure of 436,000 full-time equivalent) then only 15% of the estimated Russian supply of qualified scientists and engineers were engaged in research. If all the 'project and design' scientists and engineers are excluded, the figure is 13%.

Following discussions with members of the Russian State Committee on Science and Technology and officials in the Ministry of Education, I have certain reservations about these calculations. I formed the impression that the appropriate figure for qualified scientists and engineers employed in RandD is in the region of 500,000 (which would presumably fall within the limits estimated by Davies, Barker, and Fakiolas for 1962), but that the total supply of employed qualified scientists and engineers was less than the 3,176,000 given for 1962. It is of course difficult to be certain that the translation from their concept of scientist to our concept of qualified scientist and engineer was accurate, and I simply record an impression that, as we define the categories, the proportion of scientists and engineers employed in RandD is in the region of 20%.

We were of course interested in the methods used to make education 'responsive to social needs', and in particular in their methods of forecasting the need for various quantities and types of scientists and engineers. The Minister of Education summed up the state of the art in Russia in the remark that if any one discovered how to do such a forecast he would be made a Member of the Russian Academy before he had even taken his Doctorate. Their methods of forecasting appear to be no better than ours.

2. EXPENDITURE ON RESEARCH AND DEVELOPMENT

It is extraordinarily difficult to compare Russian expenditure on RandD with that in the West. It is not clear just how far expenditure on project-design organizations is included in the official statistics (although it is clear that not all of it is included), and it is therefore not clear what figures of research expenditure correspond to the RandD qualified-manpower estimates of 416,000 and 487,000. It is more difficult to extract research expenditure in the social sciences and the humanities, than it is to extract the manpower. The Soviet definition of national income excludes services and therefore differs from our GNP. And finally, because of a very different cost and price structure, the calculation of a research rate of exchange is subject to an unusually wide margin of error.

The expenditure on RandD as defined in the West is thought to have been between 4·1 and 5·0 billions of new roubles in 1962 (depending mainly on whether part of the assumed project and design expenditure is included). At 4·3 billions, the figure used by Davies and colleagues, RandD was 2·6% of the Soviet measure of national income, and about 3% on the Western measure of GNP at factor cost. This compares with 2·8% of GNP for the United States (using the recently revised statistics) and 2·3% for the United Kingdom in the same period.

The GNP of the United States is considerably higher than that in Russia. However a 'research rouble' would purchase more RandD inputs in terms of dollars than is suggested by the official currency rate of exchange of 1 rouble to 111 cents. Davies and colleagues tentatively suggest that the appropriate research rate of exchange is in the range of 1 rouble = $2·50–3·50. At $2·50 to the rouble, the Russian RandD expenditure in 1962 was $10,250 million–$12,500; at $3·50, $14,350 million–$17,500 million. This is a very wide range indeed – the lowest figure being 60%, and the highest 110%, of the United States expenditure ($15,610 million) in 1962. Using a research exchange rate of $5 to £1, the implied Russian expenditure was three to five and a half times the United Kingdom expenditure. There is ample room here for 'optimists' and 'pessimists' who ignore limits of error to conduct a heated debate. Light without heat may be all moonshine but in this case no one could tell on which side the sun was shining.

3. UNIFORM TECHNOLOGY

Given the Russian emphasis on central planning and the ideological objection to 'market forces', the emphasis given to a uniform technological policy is not surprising. Plans for new technology have been included in the national economic plans for almost twenty years. Central control over capital expenditure, and the central choice of input-output norms for planning purposes, provide the means for the application of this policy. Although the Russian economic system differs greatly from our own, with the creation of a Ministry of Technology, implying a decision to give greater emphasis to the role of the State in forcing a more rapid application of science and technology in industry, an examination of Russian procedures has acquired an additional interest.

The concept of a uniform technological policy is far from straightforward. Does the concept apply only to the installation of new plant over fairly short periods of time? Is the most economic plant the same in all regions? Does the concept imply centralization of R and D? If so, how are the problems which arise out of the separation of R and D from the management of the enterprises solved? Has the emphasis on this central planning of new technology and input-output norms left the managers of enterprises with sufficient incentive to improve their industrial housekeeping? Has the complicated system of success indicators created any lack of enthusiasm for innovation?

The new technology section of the Plan has several distinct parts to it – instructions to cease production of certain types of obsolete machinery, directives as to the quantity of new industrial products, the development and proto-type production of new machines, and the most important lines of R and D.

In preparation for the 1966–70 Plan the State Committee prepared a paper on 'Principal Trends in the Development of Science, and Programme of Scientific & Technological Problems for 1966–70'. The paper is divided into three sections: Natural and Social Sciences; Principal Tasks in the Development of Technological Progress in the National Economy; and Branches of the National Economy.

The first section, on Science, outlines a wide range of general and specific problems in physics, chemistry, biology, and geology. Of particular interest in this context are the references to mathematics and economics. The goal set for theoretical and applied mathematics is 'the development of the mathematical foundation of computer technology and automation, of modern advanced computers, the theory of industrial process control, and mathematical models forming the basis of the optimization of planning and control of the national economy'. For economic science it is said that special attention must be concentrated on the further development of the theoretical foundations of the planned management of the economy based on a profound understanding and extensive application of the laws of socialism, of increased general productivity, the use of economic stimuli, the improvement of methods of planned price formation, a rational distribution of the resources of production and manpower, the study and application of the benefits of an international division of labour.

The second general section on Technology, ranges from very general objectives such as 'the development and widespread introduction of new high productivity technological processes, ensuring further intensification of industry, improvement in the quality of industrial products, reduction in the labour and material costs and integrated utilization of natural resources and raw materials', to rather more specific objectives such as the application of modern computer and communication techniques to national economic planning and industrial control, and the planning and development of a national system for the dissemination of scientific and technological information.

The third section dealing with branches of the national economy is rather more specific, but still for the most part very general. The specific references include the introduction of 200 and 300 MW thermal power stations; the production of more economic power units of 500, 800 MW, and larger units; installation of water turbines of up to 500–550 MW; the introduction of 750 kv AC transmission lines; the construction of overland gas pipe lines using large diameter pipes; completing the change-over from narrow-seam mining of coal; the extensive introduction of tyre manufacture technologies improving the service life of tyres by a factor of 1·5 compared to 1965 tyres; the introduction of automated computerized accounting and control systems on all types of transport; the use of critical path planning and computer techniques to reduce building times. General references include improvements on boring and drilling technology, the design, development, and widespread introduction of new high productivity equipment for continuous casting and rolling of light metals, improvements in the quality, reliability, and service life of engineering products and drastic improvements in manufacturing technologies; production and introduction of new high productivity machinery and equipment in all branches of the national economy, ensuring complex integrated mechanization of industrial processes; the development of scientific foundations for the control of agriculture.

It is clear that much of this could not be closely co-ordinated with other parts of the National Plan. It is also clear that the Russians are not satisfied with the present position. The Director of the Institute of Economics of the Academy of Sciences said recently that the planning of scientific and technical progress is the weakest link in the whole complex of economic planning and in the whole system of material incentives for production.

During our discussion with members of the State Committee on Science and Technology, I mentioned certain factors which delay the application of science and technology to industry in the United Kingdom: the invention of new products or processes which it was uneconomic to use, often caused by the isolation of R and D from production; lack of receptivity on the part of management owing to incompetence, ignorance, or lack of incentive to innovate; and special labour problems. We received a very emphatic reply that all three factors are also important in Russia, a reply which went some way to answering the questions posed above. However they appeared to be very hopeful that the economic reforms announced by Kosygin would improve matters.

4. THE KOSYGIN REFORMS

The 1965 reforms were concerned partly with cancelling Khrushchev's 1957 reforms, and partly with a cautious experiment in 'Liberman-ism'. In 1957 the highly centralized system of thirty Industrial Ministries was replaced by over one hundred regional economic councils. This was meant to remove ministerial barriers between industries and to facilitate regional co-operation between different branches of industry. At the same time the country was divided into seventeen large planning regions controlled by Gosplan to provide for a central co-ordination of the regional economic councils. These reforms did not produce the desired effects – they induced a drive to regional self-sufficiency, a tendency to over ambitious regional investment plans and a non-uniform technological policy in regional sections of the same industry. In an attempt to deal with these new problems, in 1962–3 the number of regional economic councils was halved, an all-Union economic council was set up to control them, control over major capital investment was centred in Gosstroi, and several State Committees were created with some of the technical and planning functions of the former Ministries. With the growth in scale, variety, and emphasis on innovation, the problems of communication and decision multiply rapidly. Neither the new Khrushchev administrative structure, nor the tests of success applied to enterprises were likely to create conditions for the effective communication of information to those making the key decisions.

In September 1965 the regional economic councils and the industrial state committees were abolished and operational control of the industrial enterprises was again vested in industrial Ministries. Gosstroi remained responsible for capital investment in major construction, a new State committee Gossnab was given overall responsibility for the allocation of materials, the renamed State Committee for Science and Technology was given greater powers to co-ordinate R and D, and Gosplan, Gosstroi, Gossnab, and the State Committee were all made directly responsible to the Council of Ministers.

These definite centralizing administrative reforms were accompanied by promises of greater autonomy to enterprises in the choice of methods of production and the product mix, encouragement of direct contracts and association between enterprises, a reform of the pricing system so that all reasonable successful enterprises would be able to make profits, and, following this, the substitution of sales and profits tests for the present complex assortment of success indicators.

In discussions leading up to the announcement of this reform, considerable emphasis was given to the information problem. The 'cybernetics group' took the view that the development of computers has so transformed the information-decision problem that it is now both feasible and advantageous to centralize the economy still further. Others argued that although mathematical models and computers have an important part to play in working out an outline plan, socio-economic life is too complex to lend itself to complete description and control of the type required for computerization. In announcing the reforms Mr Kosygin (an ex-Gosplan man) made no mention of the application of computers to planning. However, earlier this year (1966) it was decided to set up a State computer network to collect and process information and to help in the formulation of plans.

Gosplan officials were very cautious in their remarks about the proposed function of Gosplan under the new arrangements. We were given a good deal of well-known information – that Gosplan's most detailed plans cover only about 1,000 key products, and that its long-term plans deal with only 400 to 500 products; that the plans of the Ministries are much more detailed and are agreed in detail with the relevant supply authorities; that Gosplan's task is to ensure that the Ministries' plans are consistent with balance in the main sectors of the economy. Some emphasis was given to the fact that although the Ministries control production and deal with issues of technical policy, etc., Gosplan employs many engineers and its plan contains a special section devoted to technological development; that issues of technical progress are very important when agreeing plans for capital expenditure, and that Gosplan brings into account the opportunities of technical progress when fixing the plans for production costs. We learned very little about the division of responsibility between Gosplan and the State Committee, though we were informed by Academician Kirillin that disagreements between Gosplan and the State Committee were taken to the Council of Ministers only if they concerned the all-Union Plan – 'otherwise we would lose our way'.

We did not get the impression that the 'uniform technological policy' was to be changed. Indeed one of the objections to the 1957 reforms was that they impeded innovation via central planning and administrative pressure. Whereas until 1957 the key control was exercised by the project-making organizations responsible to the Ministries, after 1959 these project-making organizations functioned under diverse authorities. But, as we have seen, the results were judged to be unsatisfactory, and in 1962 Gosstroi and the State Committee were given responsibility for the project organizations. The responsibility is now with Gosstroi and the Ministries.

5. INVESTMENT CRITERIA

In 1958 a conference on problems of determining the economic effectiveness of capital investment and new technology was held under the sponsorship of the Institute of Economics of the Academy of Sciences and the Economics Committee of the Central Council of Trade Unions. The recommendations published by the Academy of Sciences in 1960 (*Tipovoya Metodika . . .*) were cleared with Gosplan and other interested agencies, but so far as I know, they have never been made binding on those responsible for project appraisal. The method recommended was the 'co-efficient of relative effectiveness' (CRE).

e, the economy in operating expenditure per rouble of additional capital outlay, equals $(C_b - C_a)/(K_a - K_b)$, where C_a and C_b represent the annual operating cost (including depreciation) of two alternative projects for producing the same output and K_a and K_b the corresponding capital outlays.

Suppose $K_a = 100$, $K_b = 60$, $C_a = 50$, and $C_b = 60$. In this case $e = \frac{1}{4}$. e is the reciprocal of the 'period of recoupment'. If 10 years is set as the minimum period of recoupment then E, the standard CRE, $= 1/10$. In this case, because $1/e < 1/E$, and $C_a + E K_a < C_b + E K_b$, project A will be preferred.

Where capital outlays are not all made in the initial period and operating costs are not constant over time, then the CRE criterion, $C + E K = $ minimum, can be reformulated (as in the Academy of Sciences publication *Tipovoya Metodika . . . .*)

$$\sum_{n=0}^{N} (C + K)(1 + E)^{-n} = \text{minimum},$$

where E serves as the rate of discount.

At Gosplan and the State Committee we were informed that decisions on new technology were made on combined economic and technical tests. We were also assured that capital investment is concentrated in those industries where opportunities for technical progress are greatest. It was said that normally the criterion used is period of payback. However this period was said to be 'normally 2 to 10 years' (after provision for standardized rates of depreciation). The normal payback or recoupment periods mentioned in *Tipovoya Metodika . . .* were 10 years for energy and transportation, 6 to 7 for construction and metallurgy, 3 to 5 for chemicals machinery and coal, and 3 for light industry. It seems that this is still roughly the situation.

In most East European countries, E is not now differentiated by branches of industry. There has recently been some discussion of the issue in Russia. It is agreed, I think, that the present price structure is not a useful basis for a uniform E, but there is still not agreement on whether E should be standardized after price reform. I was informed 'that those people who want payback periods to remain strongly differentiated reflect the practice of planning in Russia and that this practice is not likely to change markedly in the near future'.

It is said, however, that when the whole economy is switched over to the new system by 1968, approximately 20% of investment will be decentralized. We asked Gosplan officials how this would affect their power to plan the economy. We were informed that Gosplan is very much in favour of the new system – that much of the detail with which they have been burdened in the past will be shifted on to the shoulders of the enterprises. In the future, it was said, Gosplan would only have to worry about the main proportions of the economy, it would be able to give much greater attention to the quality of plans as well as to the problems of regional planning.

In the past, decisions to decentralize investment have never, in practice, gone very far, because of the central allocation of materials and the uniform technological policy. As these will remain, it would seem that the extent of decentralization will depend on achieving a price reform that will both make it possible to operate general controls over the economy and give an incentive to enterprises to adopt new technologies.[1] As things stand at the moment, I was told, there are cases where it pays enterprises to buy 'obsolete' rather than modern machines because the greater capital cost was not compensated by smaller running cost. When I pointed out that according to the recoupment formula firms should act in this way, I was informed that the trouble was that it was customary to fix the price of new machines on the basis of first costs of production, and that although this was meant to be a provisional price set for 1 to 2 years in practice it tended to remain. It was said that as links between users and producers developed provisional prices would not last as long, but obviously if the first price (based on the early costs of production) discourages use, the problem will be more difficult to solve and the impetus to central administrative pressure will remain. There have been since 1960 special schemes for relieving the costs of new machines of the expenses incurred at the development stage, but I did not find how far this relief has been extended. In any case the engineering design bureaus, which employ about half a million people and have a budget of 900 million roubles, have recently been attacked for conservatism. How far this conservatism results from the critics' use of purely engineering criteria (in the absence of a reasonable price-cost system) and how far from the conservatism of enterprises I did not discover.

In September 1965 a prices committee under Gosplan was instructed to prepare a new set of wholesale prices to conform as closely as possible to socially necessary labour costs and to ensure every normally working enterprise a reasonable profit without raising retail prices. The Chairman of this Committee has announced that he does not favour any major change in the principles of price formation, and that price should equal average cost of production in the industry. This implies the need for changes in relative wholesale prices, for whereas industries such as chemicals, oil, and engineering now show profits of 30%, other industries such as coal make losses.

L

During our discussions in Gosplan we were informed that Gosplan is able through wholesale prices to regulate production. It is known that in the Russian price reform of 1961–2, cost-pricing principles were departed from in the case of oil and coal, on the grounds that unless the relative price of oil was raised there would be excess demand for it in relation to planned refining capacity. We asked whether there was to be greater use of short-term wholesale price changes to influence the pattern of resource use but we were assured that this would not be. However, in informal discussions about the use of the price mechanism, I was given an example of how this can be done in the case of new machinery. In agriculture, for example, the desire is to get the price of agricultural machinery down to encourage its use. It was said that the rate of interest charged ('averages 6% but varies')* was not reduced, but that the industry could be helped by: (i) reducing budgetary charges on the industry; and (ii) financing the investment from state funds, in which case no interest would be charged until the enterprise had reached capacity in about three years. In the Russian economy, it is more than normally difficult to distinguish between economic principles and administrative procedures.

6. NEW TECHNOLOGIES IN PLANNING?

In view of the views expressed by the Cybernetics Group in Russia and our Ministry of Technology interest in computers, we inquired about the use of computable models in planning. When we put this question to Gosplan officials, we were told that great importance is attached to mathematical models, but that it would be a relatively long time before mathematical methods could be fully used. There was some disagreement about whether the mathematical problems had been solved, but no disagreement that plans worked out from mathematical models were less accurate than the plans worked out by the traditional iterative process; and that the main problem was to get accurate data quickly enough. Here it was thought that the proposed computer network would make a big difference. (Mr Pugachev, Deputy Head of the Department for the Introduction of Mathematical Techniques in Planning, commented that although the application of mathematical methods in the socialist economy was very promising the method had to be fully built into the existing

---

* Before the reform, credits for approved modernization schemes were said to be charged at 3%.

system. In the socialist system, economic planning required a high degree of accuracy and, as distinct from the West, the mathematical system was up against great competition from existing systems!)

Where mathematical methods had been used with success was in the use of linear programming for fuel balances in different sections, the forecasting of consumer expenditure patterns, and the use of input-output analysis at the initial stages of planning.

Input-output analysis for planning was first developed in Russia in 1926, when a table of interbranch relations was computed for 1923 and 1924. Work ceased shortly afterwards and was only taken up again in 1956. In the literature, several different explanations have been suggested for the discontinuance. The Gosplan explanation was that neither the level of economic studies nor the level of technology was sufficiently advanced. Methodological studies were undertaken from 1959, and the Council of Ministers then entrusted the Central Statistical Department (which had been detached from Gosplan) with the job of interbranch balance analysis. This was done in 1960 for 1959. After this the Gosplan Research Institute started work on interbranch balances for future years. This work is very detailed and is not limited to final balances.

The first long-term interbranch balances were worked out in the Institute in 1962, and afterwards balances were worked out in physical terms for 1963, 1964, and 1965. It had been done on the largest scale yet for the five-year period 1965–70. One of the major problems in interbranch balancing was to set up a system of technically based economic norms. More than a hundred research institutes of different branches of industry took part in this work, each institute working out for its own industry norms for capital investment, and the use of capital, labour, and materials. At the same time the Institute worked on a hypothesis for the structure of the national economy. A branch balance could be worked out after bringing together this work on norms and work on the national income. Norms were worked out for expenditure on materials, fuel, labour, energy per unit of production both in physical terms and cost terms. Norms were based on those for individual enterprises, then averaged and amended to take into account likely structural changes in the national economy in the forthcoming period. Because long-term plans were worked out by Gosplan one and a half years before the plan period concerned, they could take into account the figures for capital investment and the State Committee's technological projects.

After aggregating for the main industries and agriculture, the efficiency of proposed investments can then be calculated. Members of the Gosplan Research Institute conveyed the impression that this calculation of proposed-investment efficiency was a fairly scientific business which was fully reflected in the finally agreed plan. However, shortly afterwards we were told that, because Gosplan did not know the reserves held by enterprises, they planned on the assumption that plans would be over-fulfilled. We were assured that this discrepancy would be removed under the new economic system, though just how was not made clear. It has often been suggested that, because of the size of stocks held by enterprises, something like an industrial old-boy network has grown up within Russian industry, and there is some reason to believe that the emphasis in the 'Kosygin reforms' on direct contracts between enterprises and the greater role of associations of enterprises is simply a formal recognition of this.

These measures are also meant to help solve the growing problem of consumer demand. In both Gosplan and Gosplan Research Institute, we found a frank recognition of weaknesses in the plan outcome for consumer goods. Gosplan officials after describing their techniques for forecasting consumers' demand went on to stress the importance of the reforms by which factories were put in closer touch with the trading organizations, so helping them to respond more quickly to changes in demand. We were also informed in the Gosplan Research Institute that 'Gosplan is good at industrial planning only'. Clearly Gosplan has not been successful in agriculture, and there have been considerable shortcomings in the consumer-goods sector. But the comment may have had a rather more extended reference. Gosplan does not use the levers to control overall demand for resources. The flows of output and expenditure are supposed to be kept in balance at a constant price level. Gosplan calculates this balance in association with the Ministry of Finance and the State Bank, but is not very good at it.

It is not very surprising that in announcing the reforms Mr Kosygin, a former Chairman of Gosplan, did not mention the application of computers to planning. Although planning techniques are becoming more sophisticated, there is much to be done before the potentialities of the modern computer can be harnessed to the planning task.

7. TENTATIVE CONCLUSIONS

It would be foolish for a non-Sovietologist to reach any firm conclusions after a very short visit. But for what they are worth here are some general observations about the likely significance of the Kosygin reforms.

(*a*) The Kosygin reforms include some sensible changes in working rules which will improve the working efficiency of enterprises, particularly in the consumer goods sector[1].

(*b*) The actual changes in the planning system will depend in some measure on the price reform, which has not yet been agreed. So far as I could judge, given the degree of suppressed inflation in the economy and the intention to keep the wholesale price index stable, the price reforms likely to be adopted will neither dramatically improve the communication problem between the enterprises and the central decision bodies, nor create the conditions for extensive decentralization of decisions.

(*c*) The main investment decisions will still be made centrally. The implications of the announced intention to work to a situation where 20% of investment in industry will be financed from industries' own funds do not appear to have been studied in detail. It is proposed that an enterprise, if it finds a customer for some proposed product, should be able to get credits to finance the production. But the credits will only be granted by the bank if it is satisfied that the resources are available. Materials allocation is still to be centralized and I suspect that the consequent loosening of central control will be small.

(*d*) The policy of uniform technology, which has exercised a strong centralizing influence, is not to be changed. I did not get the impression that ways had been found to integrate scientific, technological, and economic planning, more closely. As the level of technology comes closer to that in the West, this will lead to an increasing number of problems.[2]

REFERENCES

1. *The Economist* of 11th June, 1966, carries an article by the Chief Economist of the Kosino Factory, one of the forty-three enter-
L*

prises which went over to the new system in January 1966. (The number in May was 250.) The central instructions now relate to the volume of products to be sold, the nomenclature of products, the wage fund, the ratio of profit to assets employed, and tax. The factory is free to determine the product mix – it can now discontinue an obsolete line without permission – and to fix wages for (and numbers within) different categories of workers. Prices are still fixed centrally and no mention is made of the portion of profits which can be devoted to investment.

2. In a study of 'Comparative Progress in Technology, Productivity and Economic Efficiency' prepared for the Joint Economic Committee of Congress of the United States (1966), M. BORETSKY argues that in the USSR actual has been much less than feasible technical progress; that the tremendous opportunities for inexpensive borrowing and of modern technology and for capital embodied technical progress have not been exploited. Despite a lower level of technology and a very much higher investment rate, the technical progress component (as calculated by Boretsky, using the same method as for Table 4 of Chapter IX above) was very little higher in the USSR than in the United States for 1950–62:

Country	Average annual Contribution to % growth of GNP, 1950-62		
	Labour	Capital	Technical progress
USSR	1·3	3·2	1·8
USA	·8	1·0	1·7
West Germany	1·5	1·7	4·1
Italy	1·1	1·1	4·0
France	0·4	1·1	3·2
UK	0·5	0·9	1·2

I suspect that Boretsky's conclusion would be considerably strengthened if the technical progress component were adjusted to allow for structural shifts of resources from low to high productivity sectors. Although in the United States and the United Kingdom this effect was insignificant, in France, Italy, and West Germany it explained about 20% of technical progress. The percentage may have been higher in Russia.

XII

The Role of Research and Development Institutes in Applying Science to Industry*

To reduce the risk of a misunderstanding of what I will say about industrial R and D institutes, I will first attempt to make clear (i) what I mean by terms such as *science, research, technology,* and *development,* and (ii) my attitude to their roles in economic growth.

By *science* I mean the sum total of systematic and formulated knowledge about the natural world. *Research* is an activity directed towards extending this sum total of knowledge. Industrial research is an activity directed towards increasing that part of scientific knowledge likely to have application to industry, whether in the form of new (or better) products or processes.

Sometimes the new knowledge yielded by industrial research can be applied directly to industry. Thus a manufacturing fault may be referred to the research scientists who may be able to provide an explanation and a solution. For example, in early graphite-moderated gas-cooled nuclear reactors, the graphite gave trouble from the outset. In certain reactor conditions, distortion of the graphite's crystal structure can seriously alter its dimensions and lead to internal stresses which can be involuntarily released with evolution of heat. Once scientists came to understand this phenomenon, it was possible to rearrange reactor design to avoid the difficulty.[1]

Frequently, however, the results of research cannot be applied directly to industry. A further example from the same graphite-moderated gas-cooled reactors will make this clear. At high temperatures and under neutron irradiation, graphite is chemically attacked by the carbon dioxide used as a coolant. The problem may be solved by making the graphite moderator part of the fuel element, in which

* Written for the *Inter-regional Seminar on Industrial Research and Development Institutes in Developing Countries* organized by the UN, Beirut, 30th November to 12th December, 1964.

case the moderator would be replaced and renewed with the fuel, or by using heavy water as the moderator. In both cases, research is involved but the passage to successful application cannot be either direct or certain. Technical *development* is the process of building and testing scaled-up models of processes used in laboratory research, or prototypes based on design research. It is because the application of science to industry often contains a strong empirical element (the 'suck it and see' approach as engineers sometimes call it), that we have to make this distinction between R and D. In general, the greater the extent to which 'practice runs ahead of theory' the greater the cost and time involved in development. This is fairly ovbious in both aircraft and atomic reactors. Of course in these industries, without a very strong basis of theoretical knowledge, development scientists and engineers would have to guess wildly about what to try, and the chance of getting a profitable technological development would be small.

Technology is the sum total of formulated knowledge of the industrial arts. Development, which adds to this vast stock of knowledge, has two aspects. The first is purely technical. It consists of testing whether technical performance of something developed in a laboratory is affected by 'scaling up' and perhaps the use of different materials; or whether something 'built off the drawing board' operates as predicted.

But development cannot be purely technical. Some new ideas are not worth getting ready for production, simply because no one but a commercial idiot would want to invest in them. This would be so with a possible new product for which there was too little demand, or a possible new process more costly than an existing process. It is an important part of the development process to get a very much better idea of market and cost conditions than is possible at the research or design stage. Sometimes demand and cost studies will make it clear that projects should be dropped. Sometimes it will be thought that re-design is called for. Such re-design as the facts become clearer is a typical part of an efficient development process. Sometimes re-design will entail further research; sometimes simply the use of cheaper materials and components or a less cautious approach to capacity limits. Neglect of the commercial aspect of development can lead to investment in projects which have to be abandoned, or at least to premature, and therefore needlessly costly, investment decisions.

An interesting example both of commercial pressure to adopt a less cautious approach to design limits, and of premature innovation, at least as judged by many economists, is provided by the British nuclear power programme. In a Government White Paper of 1955 it was argued that the costs of nuclear and conventional power were about equal, and nuclear power stations were commissioned in the expectation that they would in time produce cheaper power than conventional stations could. In fact, nuclear power has proved to be more expensive. Because the capital cost per unit output is very much higher in nuclear stations, the Government calculation was very sensitive to the assumed rate of interest. The assumed rate of interest proved to be much too low. Furthermore, no allowance was made for improvements in the design of conventional stations, whereas capital costs per unit of 'sent out' capacity fell 50%. In reaction to this (and helped of course by continuing R and D work), capital costs in newly designed nuclear stations have been reduced by the same percentage. This has involved building reactors with an output capacity very much larger than those which have been tested. According to Sir Christopher Hinton,[2] these rapid advances were less supported by industrial experience than the wise engineer would wish, and not without hazard. But the competitive position of nuclear power could only be maintained by accepting these risks.

I. DEVELOPMENT GAPS

Obviously the use of science to change technology can be a very difficult and complex matter. When science is not used sufficiently to change technology it may be said that there is a development gap. A development gap, as usually defined, exists when there is a failure to develop usable research discoveries (or when one country's research results are developed in another). But since research is simply a process of adding to the vast stock of scientific knowledge, it is better to say that there is a development gap when the bridges from science to technology are inadequate.

Because it is possible for research institutes to increase the development gap, an analysis of the possible reasons for development gaps should be a useful introduction to the role of such institutes.

Development, as we have discussed it, has two parts – technical and economic. When, however, the failure, or alleged failure, to apply science to industry is explained in terms of a development gap, the discussion generally goes beyond the relation of science to technology and introduces a new part of the problem – namely, a decision to use a new technology. I have defined development as a process of finding out whether a proposed new technology is of technical and economic value. The decision to adopt a development is another matter. I define this as an *innovation*. It follows that the explanation of development gaps is a matter both of development and of investment in innovation.

In highly developed countries failure or slowness in applying science to industry may be due to:

(*a*) A shortage of qualified scientists or engineers engaged in development relative to research. This shortage may be due to an actual shortage of development scientists or engineers or to an unwillingness to invest resources in risky development projects. The cost of development is often very much greater than the cost of research and there may be a shortage of risk capital available for it.

(*b*) A failure to develop the right things. This may be due to a concentration on the technical aspects of development at the expense of the economic. If the problems of development are not correctly stated, we cannot expect development departments to produce proposals that the production and finance departments will gobble up. Whether the problems of development are likely to be posed correctly depends in large measure on the communication network, in this case between people in development, production marketing, and finance departments. An efficient network generally requires the employment of scientists and engineers outside R and D departments and of social scientists within them. This will make it more likely that the production, marketing, and financial problems will be put in the appropriate manner to the development engineers, and that the development engineers will get the appropriate answers to questions about production and market conditions.

(*c*) An inability to make use of promising, even successful, proven inventions. This failure may be due to the inability, or unwillingness, of existing managers and workers to cope with the new technology. This in turn may be due to the absence of people with the required skills or to their employment in the wrong places. There is now a good deal of evidence that in the United Kingdom economy we could increase the application of science to industry by redeploying our scientists and engineers. There are too many in research relative to development relative to production.

(*d*) A shortage of industrial risk capital. It should be made clear that this may be closely related to (*a*), (*b*), and (*c*). Amongst other things, the development process should eliminate a large number of unknowns and establish with much greater certainty the technical and economic potential. If there is under-investment in development, if development is not concerned with both technical and economic solutions, if the firm is not manned and organized to cope with changing technologies, then the risks of innovation will be needlessly high. The apparent shortage of risk capital may be largely a reflection of these other factors.

The less developed a country, the less is there likely to be a development gap problem, and the more is the problem of applying science to industry likely to centre round the supply of scientists, engineers, and technicians. The key problem is to introduce a knowledge of existing science, and of technologies that have been well and truly tried in richer countries. This does not mean that in making good use of science in industry there will be no need for any R and D. Research may be needed to produce more appropriate flora and fauna or to establish the precise nature of local industrial materials. And development may be needed to adapt technologies to different operating conditions. Different temperatures, raw materials, relative prices of factors of production, ratios of skilled to unskilled labour, etc. may call for skilled development or re-design work. But in the main poor countries do not have to go to the expanse of creating science and technology. What they most need already exists.

2. PRIORITIES IN THE USE OF SKILLED MANPOWER

It should be obvious that scientists, engineers, and technicians can be used in different ways, and that making best use of science and technology in industry involves making the best use of scientists and technologists.

The best use varies with the supply of scientists and technologists, the level of technology, and (the partly dependent) industrial structure.* If a country with a very poor supply of scientists and

* Compare in this respect the Australian and the United Kingdom economies. If, in 1961, Australia had spent on R and D the same over-all percentage of net output as the United Kingdom expenditure would have been £70 million. But based on the same percentage of net output, industry by industry, the expenditure would have been only £40 million. The main reason is that the aircraft, chemical, electrical, and precision instruments industries are relatively less important in Australia. It is worth noting that the *total* Australian supply of scientists and technologists was nowhere near sufficient to manage an R and D effort of £40 million. The Australians have made up for their poor scientific manpower position by attracting the United Kingdom and American chemical, electrical, and car manufacturers.

technologists went in for much RandD, it would in this way ensure that it could not apply science to industry. In any case with a poor supply of scientists and technologists the level of technology would almost certainly be low, and it would be possible and cheaper to advance by using technologies established in other countries. As the supply of scientific manpower and the level of technology rose, it would become economic to increase the proportion of scientists and engineers engaged in RandD. Within RandD there would also be a similar shift in priorities. The case for much research effort would first be poor, and then become stronger.

This line of argument sometimes leads to accusations of encouraging, or perpetuating, technological colonialism. As applied to former colonies with low incomes it is more to the point to argue that many colonial powers were too superficial in their cultural impact – that they did not leave behind a good supply of engineers and technicians capable of exploiting the teeming reservoir of science and technology. Among the most acute problems in poor countries is the acute scarcity of production knowhow and scientific manpower which should not be wasted on, for example, prestigious atomic energy research. This is not the place for a detailed discussion of manpower distributions.[3] Suffice to say that there is a good deal of evidence that even the United Kingdom could raise her technological level faster with a smaller percentage of QSE in RandD.[4]

In considering general RandD strategy we need to take into account more than the technological level and QSE percentage. The absolute size of the economy is also important.

There is a threshold-effect in both RandD. A certain minimum scale of expenditure, which in some industries (e.g. aircraft and atomic energy) is very large indeed, is required for effective work. In a very large economy, such as the United States, it is possible to take on a very wide range of RandD problems without running the danger of spreading resources too thinly in them all. By contrast, the United Kingdom, France, and Germany, with their smaller economies, cannot maintain an effective effort right across the board without an inefficiently thin spread of effort. In other words, the smaller the economy the more selective it needs to be, unless its smallness is offset by a very high ratio of scientists and technologists to the working population. The need for selectivity applies also within a chosen field. For example, if the United Kingdom tried to work in all the potentially interesting fields of nuclear reactor development, the work would be so diffused that results would probably not be obtained in any of them.

It follows that there must be economic gains to be made from international 'trade' in science and technology. Most scientific results 'trade' at very low prices in journal form. Much technology is traded in the form of new or improved products and machines. But some is traded in the form of licences to produce or to receive 'knowhow'. Not all of this trade involves recorded money payments – there are 'barter' agreements between firms and in the case of direct investment in foreign countries the payment merged in the profits of the subsidiary company – but where it is recorded payments even by developed countries may greatly exceed receipts.

There is nothing inherently surprising in this. It is only to be expected that the principles of division of labour and specialization should apply to R and D. But the importance of international 'trade' in science and technology has not received proper recognition. That economic nationalism is a significant force in R and D expenditure is due partly to the tremendous importance of 'defence' R and D – 50% of total R and D in the United States in 1961 and 40% in the United Kingdom – and partly to the widely held belief in 'scientific circles' that the national R D rate determines the growth rate. It does not. Given the distinctions we have had to make between *science*, *technology*, and *innovation*, and the continuing differences in industrial structures and levels of technology, this is not surprising. In a general way, higher Q S E percentages and R D rates become more important conditions of growth as G N P *per capita* rises, but the present big differences between countries with similar levels of growth and *per capita* income are likely to persist.[5]

3. THE ORGANIZATION OF INDUSTRIAL RESEARCH AND DEVELOPMENT

Expenditure on industrial R and D should be thought of as inputs designed to produce useful outputs. In so far as they are useful outputs they will become inputs in some production process. Now given the time lags involved, we should think of R and D as an investment process. Optimum allocation of resources therefore involves taking investment in R and D to the point where the marginal yields from it equal yields from alternative investments. Various calculations of yields to investment in R and D have been made. Almost ten years ago R. H. Ewell estimated that for the United

States economy the net yield to RandD was between 100 and 200%
per annum. Ewell's calculations were very crude – he used bivariate
analysis in a multivariate system – and did not attempt to calculate
the marginal yields to investment in RandD. If we assume that
businessmen equate private rates of return on investment in RandD
and equipment then from the known rates of return on capital
investment, we can be confident that marginal private returns on
investment in RandD are very much lower. A recent inquiry within
Imperial Chemical Industries showed that for every £1 million
invested in research assessable yields were averaging £200,000 a year
for ten years.[7] With a time lag of two years this implies a 10%
internal rate of return, using the discounted cash flow formula

$$C = \frac{Y_1}{(1 + R)} + \frac{Y_2}{(1 + R)^2} + \ldots + \frac{Y_n}{(1 + R)^n}$$

where C is the research outlay, Y the annual yield, and R the internal
rate of return.)

If we look at RandD in this sort of way, there may seem no
reason why it should be treated any differently from any other form
of investment; no reason, that is, why in a market economy RandD
should not be left to market forces.

However, it is necessary to look at what is counted in a market
economy. Social yields to investment in RandD may be larger than
the yields that accrue to the firms making the outlay. Yields to
investment in RandD are not certain. Many RandD projects do not
pay off. Yields to RandD programmes are more certain, *cet. par.*, the
greater the number of projects. But only large firms are able to
reduce risk by having a large basket of seemingly worthwhile projects.
Furthermore, it will generally not be possible for firms with successful
RandD outputs to make other firms pay according to benefits
received. There will, therefore, tend to be an underinvestment in
RandD in market economies, which will be greater the nearer we
approach the traditional model of perfect competition.

Where firms in a market economy are already undertaking RandD
of the socially desirable kind, but simply not in sufficient volume,
it is conceptually possible to use subsidies to lift RandD expenditures
to the right levels. It is, however, difficult in practice to make subsidies sensitive to differing size structures* and powers to appropriate

* In both the United Kingdom and the United States 350 large firms account for
over 85% of total industrial expenditure on RandD.

the social yields from RandD. Where socially desirable forms of research (for example, basic research) are just not undertaken, the subsidy method is quite ineffective.

It is worth considering whether we could achieve the appropriate levels of RandD expenditure if RandD were treated as a specialist central function. If it were undertaken by a vast RandD corporation with broad divisions reflecting the main fields of science and application, the RandD corporation would be able to spread risks in a way that individual firms cannot. It would also be able to economize scarce scientific manpower by avoiding competitive duplication,* and be in a position to reap the suspected economies of scale in research.[8] But such a corporation could not put optimal RandD programmes on a self-financing basis. It would not be able by selling RandD results to appropriate the full yields from RandD work. For the RandD institute to work on anything like a proper basis it would be necessary to give subsidies based on detailed cost-benefit analyses. Given the problems involved – the fact that RandD now will produce its yields in the future (if at all), the difficulty of determining appropriate time discount rates to value contributions to yield in the future, the difficulty of isolating the effects of RandD in relation to education in relation to organization changes etc.[9] – it would be foolish to imply that we would be able to recognize the precise socially desirable RandD programme even if we met it. The difficulty exists whatever the form of organization. But there are special difficulties relating to the proposal to centralize RandD. It was suggested above that there are economies of scale which such an institute could reap. This is probably true. But given the possibility of dis-economies of scale for other reasons the real question is whether there would be *net* economies of scale.

The distinction between basic research, applied research, and development is not always clear-cut. But often it does reflect differences in appropriate forms of organization. It is often said that research needs to be free of any external direction or organization, that the key to successful research is the unpredictable creativeness of individuals and that 'in running a research establishment one is really running a gambling concern and taking incalculable risks for unassessable rewards'.[10] It is true that in basic research there can seldom be any question of organizing to create a *particular* result. This is a major explanation of the eminence of universities in the

---

* I should have said, more realistically, 'reducing competitive duplication'. There is often secrecy and competitive duplication within firms and institutions.

fields of basic research. But as we move further through the stages of applied R and D, organization for a particular result becomes not only possible but essential.

Efficiency in industrial research is largely a matter of choosing the right problems. There are thousands upon thousands of possible research projects – the crucial task is to choose those few projects which are made relevant by the market position, the financial resources, the production problems, and the management skills of the firms and industries.

In development, which is frequently many times more expensive than the preceding research, there is a still greater need to relate the choice of projects and the precise objectives of the development team to production problems, available finance, and the market opportunities of the firms or institutions for which the invention is being developed. Here detailed team work and organization is essential. 'For instance, it is often true in the chemical industry that at the pilot-plant stage the main problems are already known, and the remaining work can be foreseen in fair detail. This makes it possible to organize a co-ordinated attack along several lines at once assigning workers their specific tasks. A tighter organization is also needed at the development stage to prevent waste of time later. The technical solution coming forward from the scientists has to be re-lated to the production and marketing problems of the firm. Unless the production and sales staff have a chance to express their views during development, they may bring forward important new points when investment for full-scale production is in progress. There is a temptation for production engineers, if they have not been consulted earlier, to try to improve on the fully developed design, and this is a frequent cause of delay in commercial operation.'[11]

It is almost impossible for large R and D institutes to be close enough to production and marketing problems to conduct final development efficiently. Such institutes can very easily magnify the development gap problem.

Of course, where research creates the possibility of an entire new industry, the problem cannot be posed in this way. When the United Kingdom Government set up the Atomic Energy Authority it was entirely appropriate to ask it to take charge of the research into and development of nuclear reactors. But now that nuclear reactors have been put into commercial operation, the position has changed. To continue to centralize reactor development in the Atomic Energy Authority could lead to them spending vast sums on developing types of reactor design which are not appropriate to the plans of the Central Electricity Generating Board.

There is no reason to believe that there are net economies of centrally organized R and D and there is particularly little reason to believe so of development. Owing largely to problems of communication and differing objectives, there are economies of specialization within this vast field. But what of much more limited forms of specialization? I will approach this question obliquely by giving a brief outline and appraisal of the British organization of R and D.

4. THE BRITISH CASE

The United Kingdom is a wealthy country, with a large supply of scientists and technologists and a distinguished record in scientific discovery. Yet for the last sixty years there has been concern about the alleged failure of industry to apply science. In 1900 the National Physical Laboratory was established 'to bring scientific knowledge to bear practically upon our everyday industrial and commercial life, to break down the barrier between theory and practice, to effect a union between science and commerce'. The National Physical Laboratory is now part of the Department of Scientific and Industrial Research (D S I R) which was established in 1916. To match Germany in applying science to industry it was thought necessary to have State assistance to promote and organize scientific research with a view especially to its application to trade and industry. At a time when industrial R and D hardly existed in the United Kingdom, D S I R was expected to: (i) encourage individual firms in science-based industries to do research; (ii) help form, and (until they were firmly established) subsidize, co-operative research associations (R A's) on an industry basis, where (because firms were too small to organize and finance a research department and/or the research required was too long-term) research would not pay individual firms but would pay the industry; and (iii) undertake socially useful research which would not pay industry.

There certainly has been a tremendous increase in R and D conducted by individual firms – it now costs more than 3% of industrial net output. In 1961 the United Kingdom's total expenditure on R and D was £634 million, of which 58% was spent by private industry. However, 40% of industry's R and D was financed by the Government, mostly by defence R and D contracts of over £150 million. Private industry's own-financed R and D was only

33% of total RandD, though 55% of all RandD for civil purposes. As we have seen, most of this RandD is conducted by 350 large firms in a few modern industries.

There are now about sixty co-operative RAs. Fifty-two receive subsidies from DSIR, which in total provides 25% of their income. The original belief that DSIR would only need to 'prime the pump' proved incorrect. Grant aid is given, however, in proportion to the sums raised from industry.

Co-operative research is not restricted to small-firm industries: there is a Motor Industry RA, a Cement RA, an Iron and Steel RA, and (until recently when it was amalgamated with Cotton and Silk) a Rayon RA. But most are in the small-firm industries, such as pottery, wool, linen, lace, felt, glue, cutlery, etc.

The RAs have done very valuable work, though they are now responsible for a very small part of industrial RandD – 3% of civil RandD in industry (compared to over 6% in 1946). Whereas their expenditure increased 65% between 1955 and 1961, private industry's (own-financed) RandD increased over 200%.

Why has co-operative research not grown faster? In 1961, on average, their expenditure was divided as follows: 23% basic research, 47% applied research, 18% technical liaison, and 12% library and information. RAs are most successful where they serve industries with relatively large firms. For such firms employ scientists and engineers who can develop the RA ideas for their own use, in contrast to many small firms which cannot even understand the concepts and terminology used in technical literature. Here the 'communication loss' is a serious one. For the small firms the most important thing is technical advice on the lines used successfully in agriculture. This underlines the points made earlier about the distribution of scientific manpower and the close relations between final development and actual production. But it should be emphasized that the RA movement has played an important part in inducing development work and, given that development is generally more expensive than research, the more successful it is in priming the pump in this way, the more will its *share* in industrial RandD fall. It should certainly not be thought that the RAs have failed because they have not helped to bring RandD as a percentage of net output in old-established industries up to equality with the science-based industries. Equalization of marginal returns to investment in different industries will always leave big differences in research rates.[12]

D S I R now has fifteen research stations which in 1961 spent, on basic and applied research, about the same amount as the sixty R As. Their links with industry are less direct, but they are certainly concerned with the application of science to industry. The National Physical Laboratory (which conducts a wide range of basic and applied research in aerodynamics, metallurgy, radio, optics, mathematics, electronics, ship design, and electrical engineering) and the Laboratory of the Government Chemist are older than D S I R. D S I R created the Building Research Station, the Road Research Laboratory, and the Water Pollution Research Laboratory between the wars. Since 1945 it has created several new research stations, most of which are concerned with engineering. Some of the research work has a very direct application to industry – e.g. the work of the Forest Products Research Laboratory on Kiln seasoning, of the Torry Research Station on freezing fish at sea, of the National Physical Laboratory on the design of hulls and suspension bridges, of the Hydraulics Research Station on the location and design of viaducts – and even the measurable commercial yields to their work justify their existence.[13]

D S I R has recently placed three civil R and D contracts with private firms making machine tools and electronics. This is an attempt to stimulate innovation by subsidizing neglected types of R and D and getting them undertaken by firms with an interest in final production – a method that has worked well in defence industries. However, it will be more difficult to stimulate civil innovation in this way. In defence projects the Government is the sole buyer; in civil fields it is not. However, it is a sign of a further recognition of the need to keep final development close to production.

The National Research and Development Corporation (N R D C) – a public body founded in 1949 to deal with discoveries made in Government research establishments and to secure the further development of new ideas coming to it – also gets private firms to complete development, sometimes with the encouragement of a development contract. It has so acted with electronic computers, fuel cells, Hovercraft, Dracones and hecogenin extraction for the production of cortisone.

The biggest R and D institute is the Atomic Energy Authority which spends on civil R and D alone more than three times as much as the R As and D S I R research stations together. The Atomic Energy Authority put the United Kingdom first in the field in the commercial use of nuclear power. But given the recent rapid innovations in conventional power methods, design innovations are required to get nuclear power costs down. The segregation of development in the Atomic Energy Authority, away from the construction and use of power stations, is now beginning to be a serious problem.

The general position in the United Kingdom then, is that specialist industrial research bodies between them spend just under 20% of total civil R and D. The DSIR and RA laboratories do important work in applied research, some of which can be applied directly to industry. Where development work is required it is left to industry, though recently DSIR has started a trial run with civil R and D contracts on the lines of defence contracts. Furthermore, both DSIR and the RAs exercised a pump priming effect on development work in industry. Apart from the research institutes in agriculture (which have not been discussed here) the Atomic Energy Authority is unusual in that a high proportion of its expenditure goes on producing pilot plants. As pioneers this was inevitable, but the position is likely to change as nuclear reactor industry gets more skilled and powerful.

5. SPECIAL ROLE OF RESEARCH AND DEVELOPMENT INSTITUTES IN DEVELOPING COUNTRIES

Science imports more easily than technology, but for developing countries it is the technology that is crucial. The technology exists – it does not have to be created by a native R and D effort. But the form of the technology used in richer countries – with their better supplies of administrators, scientific and technical manpower, and capital – may be inappropriate. Even the Russians, who are now well off for business administrators and scientific manpower, do not copy United States techniques but take care to keep down capital cost per unit output. Where business administrators, technical manpower, and capital, are all in short supply, still different techniques may be appropriate. In some cases they may prove to be what engineers would regard as very modern. But Professor Leontief's general prediction that automatic factories will have a greater relevance in poor than in rich economies because of lower capital and skilled labour requirements per unit of output, leaves out of account the crucial importance of the big markets and the complex management skills required to make automatic factories economically viable.

Skilled manpower will be in short supply. It will be needed for both the adaptation and operation of technologies established in developed economies. The adaptation may require some applied research into the qualities of local materials, the effects of different operating temperatures and so on. But for the most part the need will be for development engineering. To ensure this, the essential R and D institutes will need carefully defined terms of reference. For, as I have said, the main activity should not be research but engineering development and technical information services.

To keep the correct emphasis in the R and D institutes it would be wise to employ not only scientists and engineers to do technical development and information but also social scientists to analyse costs and markets and find appropriate means of 'selling' the R and D outputs. Applying science for growth requires attention to the two faces of innovation – technical and social.

For the same reason it would be wise to think in terms of institutes to serve (or create) particular industries. Because the range of outputs is vastly less in wheat, wool, milk, etc., than in engineering, electrical, and chemical industries (and the agricultural institutes can do satisfactory final development on their own experimental farms), a higher degree of specialization is required from R and D institutes in industry than in agriculture.

The appropriate procedure is to identify the industries in which investment in technological advance is likely to bring the greatest returns, and to create R and D institutes for them with facilities for constructing prototypes and pilot plants. Once operational analysis, which would of course take into account the types of manpower required for production, showed that investment in a new technology would be sound, the institute would arrange for existing manufacturing firms (or firms created for the purpose) to use it. The institute would assist in, sometimes in fact run, the first production operations, and then continue in the role of technical consultant.

In the course of time development work would be taken on by the manufacturing firms, but it might be generations before anything like the present United Kingdom balance between the work of R and D institutes and R and D departments in firms emerged. For the longer developing countries are in a position to adapt proven foreign technologies, the less there is rapid technological obsolescence in luxury industries, and the longer it takes for supplies of scientific and technical manpower to catch up with increasing demand, the more will it pay to concentrate R and D activities in institutes.

R and D institutes are not the only way of introducing new technologies. Foreign subsidiary companies and branch factories play a very important part in diffusing technology. Hitherto such diffusion from developed to developed countries[14] has been more important than diffusion from developed to under-developed countries. For an undeveloped country this way of acquiring new technology has great advantages. The foreign company relieves the state of excess demand for scarce resources by supplying the new technology, managerial skills, and (generally) capital. However, if such firms rely entirely on the R and D work of parent companies and continue to use imported labour for key technical and managerial jobs then they do little to create the conditions of self-sustaining technological change. But this does not create a good case for discouraging foreign subsidiary companies. Rather it creates a case for associating foreign companies with training programmes and for attracting them in those fields that will complement the work of the R and D institutes, established or about to be established.

The point about complementing the work of the R and D institutes is an important one. Most of the developing countries are going to be short of high-quality scientific and technical manpower for some time to come. In the United Kingdom the minimum budget for an effective industrial RA is about £25,000 a year, and where industrial development work is involved it is considerably higher. Some United Kingdom firms argue that the minimum cost of an effective R and D *department* is £100,000 a year. The position in developing countries will be different, of course, but they will certainly have to be very highly selective in their R and D programmes. Co-operation with rich countries and with other developing countries in the choice of R and D projects and the exchange of knowledge, should therefore be encouraged. At this inter-regional seminar on industrial R and D institutes it should not be necessary to labour that point!

REFERENCES

1. Sir C. HINTON, 'Nuclear Power', *Three Banks Review* (1961).
2. *ibid.*
3. *Some Factors in Economic Growth in Europe in the 1950's* (UN, 1964).
4. On the general possibility of excessive research see F. MACHLUP, *The Production and Distribution of Knowledge*, Chapter 5 (Princeton University Press, 1962).

5. In *Science, Economic Growth and Government Policy* (OECD, Paris, 1963), the relations between RD rates and *per capita* GNP are plotted. In Sweden, West Germany, France, and Australia – countries with similar *per capita* incomes – RandD as percentages of GNP, in 1961, were 1·3, 1·1, 1·0, and 0·6, respectively. This is quite a range.

6. MACHLUP, op. cit.

7. Sir R. HOLYROYD, Paper No. 637, Institute of Chemical Engineers (March 1964).

8. T. MARSCHAK, 'Strategy and Organization in a System Project Development', *The Rate and Direction of Inventive Activity* (Princeton University Press, 1962).

9. E. F. DENNISON, *The Sources of Economic Growth in the United States* (CED, New York, 1962). (The difficulties come out clearly in his attempt to put numbers to the contributions of the various factors in economic growth.)

10. J. D. BERNAL, *The Direction of Research Establishments* (HMSO, 1957), Part A, p. 1; and C. E. K. MEES and J. A. LEERMAKERS, *The Organization of Scientific Research* (McGraw-Hill, 1950).

11. C. F. CARTER and B. R. WILLIAMS, *Science in Industry*, p. 48 (Oxford University Press, 1959).

12. For the similarity in the relative research rates in the main industry groups in the United Kingdom, United States, and Hungary see *Some Factors in Economic Growth in Europe in the 1950's*, Chapter 5. See also Y. BROZEN, 'Trends in Industrial Research and Development', *Journal of Business* (July 1960); and B. R. WILLIAMS, 'Variations par Secteur dans L'Effort de Recherche-Développement en Grande-Bretagne', *Economie Appliquée* (1961).

13. Sir H. MELVILLE, *DSIR – Does It Pay Off?* (Manchester Statistical Society, 1961).
Since this chapter was written there have been substantial changes in the machinery of Government. A newly created Ministry of Technology now has responsibility for the former DSIR research stations, other than the Road Research Board which is now responsible to the Ministry of Transport, and the Building Research Station which is responsible to the Ministry of Public Buildings and Works.

14. See, for example, J. H. DUNNING, *American Investment and British Manufacturing Industry* (Allen & Unwin, 1958).

XIII

The Automatic Factory: The Age
of Harmony, Leisure and Plenty?*

We are not on the threshold of an age of fully automatic production˙
We are moving that way, but slowly. It is nonetheless important to
think about the automatic factory now; for our thinking now will
largely determine what it will be like and how long it will take to
achieve.

The title is a question. Would the growth of the automatic factory –
the actual manufacture of acceptable products without direct human
intervention – take us towards an age of harmony, leisure and plenty?
To this question three answers have been given: 'No', 'Yes', and
'It depends . . .' I will first consider these problems of the future.
Then, I will consider the probable rate of change, since our chance
to make a satisfactory adjustment to change will depend on the time
we have for it. Finally I will say something about the implications of
present developments.

A good many people, both informed and uninformed, have
attempted to appraise the possible effects of the automatic factory
and various arguments have been marshalled both for and against.

I. ARGUMENT AGAINST

The argument that the automatic factory will not benefit society may
be broken down into several theses:

(a) That the automatic factory will create technological unemployment. This thesis in a more sophisticated form is that 'if capital
investment were to increase while the need for manpower dropped,
the consequent rise of capital's share of the national income would
cause widespread unemployment and have an adverse effect on the
standard of living'.

(b) That the unemployment will create tension and discontent within
society. The bitterness and frustration of 'men without work' will

* First appeared in *The Automatic Factory* (IPE, 1955); read at the conference
of the Institute of Production Engineers, Margate, June 1955.

infect those with work, and machines will be regarded as competitors and supplanters of men.

(*c*) That the cost of change will rise greatly. A versatile machine will be more expensive than a special purpose machine and this will lead to a still greater emphasis on keeping long unchanging runs till the equipment is worn out.

(*d*) That unless all change is rigidly programmed – a programme that would entail knowledge of, or control over, acts of God, the Queen's enemies, and you and me – the system may become unstable. For in a multiple loop system unexpected events in one loop can make the whole system unstable.

(*e*) That the automatic factory will destroy its own foundations. Mass production needs long runs and it needs a mass market. This mass market was created by massing workers together in factories. The automatic factory will un-mass workers. The mass market would then have to be re-created by taking away free choice, and by positively conditioning the citizenry to fit the needs of the factories.

(*f*) That the small number of engineers with the ultimate control of these automatic factories could, by threat of pushing the stop-production button, hold society up to ransom: the ransom being control of man's consumption and habits in the interests of the machines. The automatic factory, then, will provide an open sesame to Huxley's 'Brave New World'.

(*g*) That the vast speeding up of production will produce a growing scarcity of raw materials. This scarcity will not be spread evenly between nations. This will intensify friction between nations. Add to this the discontent at home due to unemployment and it is easy to see that the push-button factory will increase the risk of a push-button war.

In any case (*h*) that the automatic control systems are similar to the nervous systems of humans and animals. In creating automatic factories we create robot machines. How can we be safe from these Frankenstein monsters?

I will not at this stage comment on these theses, except to say that acceptance of one does not entail acceptance of all. You will all have noted the influence of science fiction within my list!

2. ARGUMENT IN FAVOUR

The argument that the automatic factory will benefit society may also be composed of several theses:

M

(*a*) That the object of production is to create things for men to use or consume. Each piece of mechanization releases hands, brains, and energies for new forms of production. The continuous mechanization that constitutes an automatic factory will bring a vast increase in production per man. This is the way to create plenty.

(*b*) That mechanization releases hands, brains, and energies, which may be used to create new commodities. When after creation the new forms of production are made automatic, new room is created for still newer commodities. If men choose not to create new commodities, the labour released will not be 'unemployed'; it will be 'employed' in leisure.

(*c*) That with greater wealth there will be an opportunity for a longer and broader education. The type of skill required will, in any case, not be a narrow specialist skill; and insofar as man uses part of his potential leisure for the creation of new forms of production, there will be a vastly expanded need for R and D.

(*d*) That the automatic factory will still need the labour of skilled maintenance men and programmers. Unless production goals were never-changing and process conditions always predictable, unaided computing machines could not solve all programme problems. Thus there would be two highly skilled types of labour controlling the machines. Man would no longer be an appendage of the machine to be paced by the machines; labour would acquire a new dignity and interest.

(*e*) That without the need for mass labour supplies there will no longer be need for vast straggling conurbations. Industry will become decentralized, even rural.

(*f*) That much of the present industrial unrest exists because man is paced by the machine and performs routine tasks. The automatic factory will dispose of this problem. It will also avoid the need to mass workers together in a factory and control them through a complicated system of status and hierarchy. The problem of human relations in industry will become relatively simple. From these last three theses we should expect industrial harmony, unless the system is unstable.

(*g*) That the fact that a multiple loop system may be unstable, should not be taken as proof that the economic system would be unstable. There is a difference between the automatic factory and an economic system composed of automatically linked automatic factories. In fact, programmers will be needed in factories to exercise judgement in control of unexpected events; and State planners, aided by computing machines, could send instructions to these programmers that would correct approaching instability or quickly offset it. Planning against instability at any rate in a closed economy would be quite simple. Thus the movement of the different sectors of the economic system could also be kept in harmony.

(*h*) That with automatic control the amount of capital required to produce each unit of output tends to decline with full utilization of capital equipment or capital saving invention. This will make it easy to export capital for the development of food and raw material resources in undeveloped countries. We will thereby secure our food and raw material base at the same time as we help to raise standards of living in poorer countries. This will help towards world peace.

3. POSSIBLE OUTCOMES

And now for the 'it depends' type of answer, which I will use to comment on the preceding theses. Most of these represent *possible* outcomes – the best and the worst possibilities: they picture the dual nature of man with his continuing capacity for wisdom and folly, creation and destruction, good and evil.

I will consider these conflicting theses in terms of the three main questions posed in the title: Leisure? Plenty? Harmony?

If automatic control and operation in factories is economic, as already in some fields it is, it must increase output per man. This must increase the possibility of leisure, unless in other fields such as agriculture and services there is an offsetting increase in demand for labour. This possibility I would not in this context take seriously. It implies either that there is technical decline in non-factory production, or that the whole increase in real income was counterbalanced by expanded demand for material goods and services.

Hours of work in this country have come down from about sixty in 1860 to forty-six at present, and the age of entry to the labour market has increased. In the United States from the 1890's to 1930, an increase of 1% in hourly real wages brought a 25–33% fall in the labour offer. In other words, one-third to one-quarter of the gain was devoted to leisure.

4. THE PROBLEM OF LEISURE

What percentage of the potential leisure will be used depends on the rate at which new material wants are created. From past experience it seems quite safe to say that some part of the potential leisure will be taken. A working week of thirty hours is quite conceivable.

But we should not pitch our expectations too high. There is more work than factory work, which in the United Kingdom uses only one-third of the labour force and is falling relative to other employment. In households, schools, laboratories, and distribution, the potentialities of automatic production are very much less. In the course of time we may devote as much labour per year to training a child as we at present lavish on champion racehorses. Certainly I would expect the labour used in education to rise with growth in real income and with an increased demand for scientists and technologists in R and D and highly skilled maintenance men in production. This is likely to entail a breadth of training and therefore a length of training to which at present we do not aspire.

This expansion of education could help solve that oddly worrying problem – the problem of leisure. If society made up its mind about the object of education and also produced an education system appropriate both to the new technology and a thirty-hour week, the problem of leisure should vanish. Unfortunately there is clearly no easy and obvious solution – certainly it is beyond the scope of a 'mechanical brain' – and since the family is a basic educational unit we cannot 'simply' arrange it through schools. I would, however, expect the problem to become much easier of solution than now appears, because through automatic control and production we would get rid of the *mass* of workers in a factory and so destroy the mechanistic concepts of the functions of workers in mass production.

But what of the potential threat to leisure from robots with brains? Frankensteins and robots are very useful devices for modern parables and satires on man. But these new 'mechanical brains' can no more think than a radio can talk. If, however, some villain or lunatic of the human species *decides* to explode a hydrogen bomb – that is serious.

Saying that society will choose to take part of the potential leisure created by automatic production, implies an increase of plenty. As this way of looking at the problem biasses the case against those who argue that scarcity will be created through exhausting natural resources, I will examine that directly.

It is quite clear that some of our resources are exhaustible: indeed, all minerals. In so far as we speed up production, we bring the time of exhaustion nearer, but how near is quite another question. Our coal reserves are vastly diminished and more difficult to mine, but uranium will before long replace coal as a source of power. By the time uranium is exhausted, doubtless other minerals will have become usable. Just as we find new uses for old minerals, so we find old uses for new minerals. How long this can go on no one can say, other that at present rates of exploitation it is a very long way off.

But what of food? This is not a problem of automatic factories, unless automatic farming devices that mine the soil are introduced.

5. EFFECT ON MATERIAL WANTS

Plenty, however, is a relative term and beyond the level of subsistence a psychological problem. We live in a state of plenty if our material wants expand less than our incomes. How will the growth of the automatic factory affect the rate of growth of our material wants? Well, it depends . . .

If society is roughly equalitarian so that we are not striving madly to keep up with the Jones's; if the automatic factory is based on flexible machines and is decentralized so that we avoid danger (Section 1. *e*); if the programmers and skilled maintenance engineers with jobs that give scope for ingenuity and pride develop the personal traits of the old craftsmen; if machines are not treated as instruments in a vast competitive struggle; if, via a richer system of education, men other than saints realize the vanity of a strained pursuit of material goods – there will be plenty and a feeling of plenty.

But things could be different. There could be a vast competitive race to speed up production more and more in automatic factories; to create bigger and better purely *technical* solutions of production problems; to condition men to want more and more of the goods that were being poured off the production lines; to conquer and exploit the stars and the planets. Such an approach would not create a feeling of plenty, but a feeling of dissatisfaction.

Whether the one or the other is the outcome would depend on the institutions created to regulate economic affairs, and on society's goals or set of values.

I come now to the third question in my title. Will there be harmony? Will machines compete with men? Will there be an impassable barrier between a few controllers and the rest? Will the system be unstable? Will international relations get worse?

6. WHO WILL BE THE CONTROLLERS?

Machines can create unemployment. It is possible to envisage a situation where automatic production replaces men in a few industries, but not in others; where in the technically unprogressive industries there was no incentive to expand employment or reduce hours. In this case the potential leisure would not be willingly taken in part by all, but forced on a few in the form of unemployment. This problem of uneven growth could be solved by a statutory reduction in working hours, unless the technically unprogressive industries were faced with fierce international competition. In this case machines would compete with man, unless there was an international agreement on hours, or subsidies to the unprogressive industries, or unless the technically unprogressive industries were made progressive. This, however, is not a problem of the automatic factory as such, but of uneven rates of growth towards it. The growth problem is capable of solution – it is one of the many aspects of the 'social control of business' of which we are becoming increasingly conscious.

Will there be an impassable barrier between the controllers and the rest? There are two issues here: will the controllers be able to push the rest around, and will there be a few supremely intelligent men who understand the machines, with the rest non-entitical?

Well, who will the controllers be? Owners? Programmers? Maintenance men? People responsible for RandD? or distribution? or education? or agriculture? There may not be any owners, but there will certainly be many 'controllers', many of them outside automatic factories, and there is no reason to expect any identity of interest in, or view about, controlling 'the rest'. Furthermore, these many controllers will be interdependent. The factory controllers could not take over farming. The factory programmers might even be unable to do the maintenance! That is not to say that a society with automatic factories could not be totalitarian. It could be. But it need not be. There is nothing new about this problem. As in our present societies 'it depends . . .' Given peace, given the absence of deep depressions, this country should find it fairly easy to keep a democratic society.

7. IMPORTANCE OF INTERNATIONAL ACTION

But will depressions be avoided? Will the system be stable? In a closed economy it should be fairly easy to avoid instability (see Section 2. *g*). The main danger to stability would come from outside the economy: from serious depression abroad, or from technical progress abroad that made one or two of our main industries obsolete and uncompetitive. This is a familiar problem. As now, success will depend on agreed international action. This is the key to the solution: it is the key to the more than this, for on it also depends the chance to build automatic factories.

Will the automatic factory intensify the problem of international relations? It need not. This will largely depend on whether or not the automatic factory creates a feeling of plenty, and on whether we use part of growing real income to *help* undeveloped countries develop *their* resources (Section 2. *h*).

So, I would conclude, it all depends, and it depends on what institutions we create, what values we develop in the near future, on what time we have to see the problems emerging.

8. THE EMERGING PROBLEMS

I think we have a great deal of time to see the problems emerging. We have good reason to expect growth towards the automatic factory to take place at different rates, and in different ways, in the various industries.

The Automatic Factory in Oil Refining

The great advance towards the automatic factory in oil refining is due to a combination of technical, economic, and historical factors that is not found in older industries. For this reason the advance to an automatic factory is likely to be both more difficult and longer sustained in most other industries.

The technical reason in the case of oil refining is that, consequent on the introduction of cracking towers, refined oils are produced by a physio-chemical process that is *continuous*. Here the growth of process control was in itself the major step towards the automatic factory. (Outside the oil industry there have been, of course, extensive applications of automatic control to processing variables, such as pressure temperature flow and level, but it is only in the chemical industry that this process control itself takes us near the automatic factory stage. Automatic process control of furnaces in a pottery factory does not take it near the automatic factory stage, nor even automatic control of open-hearth furnaces for steel production.)

The economic reason is a two-fold one. In oil refining, as in certain other heavy chemicals, a vast output of a reasonably standard product is produced. There was, in addition, a tremendous *increase* in demand – a demand that could not be met with the old batch process methods. It would be quite impossible to produce the present output of refined oil with manual operation. The rapidly expanding demand gave both the incentive and monetary opportunity to introduce automatic control.

The historical reason is that there was no past to weigh down the present. Management and marketing methods were evolved along with the techniques of large-scale refining. In older industries, the growth of the automatic factory will involve quite fundamental changes in management methods that grew up with and were appropriate to non-automatic methods. Furthermore, I should add, the management problem is on the whole simpler in the processing than in the manufacturing industries.

Following this it may be useful to divide the impediments to the introduction of the automatic factory into technical, economic, and human.

The Technical Problem

I have implied that there is no technical impediment in the case of an oil refinery. Even here, however, there is still a considerable technical problem. To get the maximum yield, temperatures and pressures must be adjusted whenever the quality of the crude oil varies. This has led to thinking about end-point control, which would require both *continuous* analysis of the product and a computer capable of using analysis reports to adjust the various controls. Both the continuous analyser and the computer present significant technical problems, though these problems are simple compared with the potential problems in other industries.

In some industries the essential properties of the raw materials is not known. Where this is so, it is not possible to write out a foolproof list such as: if you find properties *a* and *b* in the material do *z*; if *c* and *d* in *y*; if *b* and *c* in *x*. It is not possible in such cases to leave the action decisions to the computer, since the computer can only solve problems that have been anticipated in its building.

Where the process of production is not continuous, it would be necessary to join up separate automatic machines into a *system* of automatic controls. Such a system might be non-linear, and as such it may be beyond the present range of computer control. Mathematicians – I hear – have not yet worked out the full theory of non-linear systems.

The Problem of Cost

(*a*) The economic problem is one of cost: what is the cost of automatic control compared to the cost of human control? In general, at the moment, it is high. The reason is fairly simple. A machine or a group of machines is more expensive when automatically controlled. This expanse is only worthwhile when output is greatly increased, but this depends on the size and stability of the market. Where the market is limited or where it is often necessary to re-tool or re-set, the expensive controls would be left idle too long for them to be economic. In general, cost rises with complexity. This also affects computer costs – the greater the complexity, the greater the possible number of situations, the greater the number of solutions or instructions to be built into it.

It may be argued that some automatic machines are capital saving. This is true, but true in a limited field. An automatic transfer machine for machining cylinder blocks, where the machining, boring, and reaming are performed within the same machine, may be cheaper than the several machines it eliminates. In this case, clearly, automatic production is economical: the cost of the machine is less, the labour cost is reduced, the output is increased and the product is more uniform. Note, however, that this transfer machine prepares cylinder blocks – it does not make a motor-car. We cannot transfer the reasoning to the whole factory. Further, even such a spectacular piece of automation is not of general application: the large single-purpose machine is relatively easy to make automatic, but it is not easy to pay for except where it can be used for a long run.

The long run of standard product, the continuous process – these are the conditions that most favour the growth of the automatic factory. But they are not typical of industry. We do find, however, pieces of work that favour automatic control even in industries dominated by short runs, and lest I should seem to be too negative, I will now say something about them.

(*b*) 'Pieces of automation' that are economic are many. One very important example is that of the automatic quality control that has grown out of 'instrumentation'. If a product must be produced to fine tolerances, as is the case, for example, with turbine and compressor blades for modern jet engines, and if the production cycle is short, the cost of letting a machine run out of control is great. Here the cost of automatic control can soon be paid for in work not spoilt and in the equipment no longer needed to produce only a sample of good work. Fast and continuous inspection and control, whether of turbine blades or a set of dials and knobs for boilers, is beyond human beings. In such cases the high quality is only made possible by the instrumentation and automatic control. In other cases, such as atomic energy where the work is too dangerous for humans, automatic controls are equally indispensable.

These automatic quality controls, it will be noticed, are not labour replacing. They add to what labour can do: they extend the range of production and make possible the employment of new labour released, say, by transfer machines.

In other cases, pieces of automation become economic because of the scarcity of labour. Thus automatic handling and machine loading devices have become increasingly economic with the post-war shortage of labour. That there is a shortage of labour for handling and loading is itself a sign that labour has more urgent uses, many of which were provided through new activities made possible by automatic quality control. We may expect some further autonomous inventions that will be labour saving, but as these may be balanced by the desire to take more leisure with an increase in real income, I do not expect any significant new labour displacements by these 'pieces of automation'.

Human Impediments

Just as there are human efforts directed towards the creation of the automatic factory, so there are human impediments. I mention three.

(*a*) *Fear.* Fear is one of the many causes of stupidity. There are certain fears about the development of automatic controls, which if not allayed, will delay applications which are both technically and economically possible.

Management may fear that automatic controls will bring an excessive level of overhead cost or a host of technical problems that will be unmanageable. Whether automatic controls will produce 'excessive' overheads will depend on the type of control. Some of this fear results from thinking too much in terms of devices such as the transfer machine, which has only special application. Of more general application are automatic copying lathes, handling and machine loading devices, and quality controls. Such controls, by bringing fuller utilization of equipment, or by reducing waste, cut down the 'burden' of overheads.

The fear that there will be a host of rather 'unmanageable' technical problems may have some basis. The problem of maintenance will increase, and the type of management needed will change – but the problems are only unmanageable in terms of *present* management and labour skills. Even now, applications of automatic control are hindered by the shortage of technicians. This was to be expected. With a sudden growth in demand for new technical skills, demand must for a time outrun supply. Certain shortages, however, may continue – engineers with sufficient mathematical knowledge to do creative work in control systems and design engineers with the ability to re-design products in terms of the potentialities of automatic control. Change in the type of manager and management is also to be expected with change in the production problem.

Labour fears of unemployment may lead to demands that jobs be guaranteed, that redundant workers be attached to new machines, or that new methods be not introduced. In some firms this fear may have no basis; in others this fear can be calmed by guaranteeing employment – by providing for redundancy through retirement and retarded recruitment. But this will not be possible in every case. Technical progress, whether it involves automation or not, always brings with it redundancy in one place, shortage in others. If the community is to profit from the technical progress, some must change jobs. Because the fear of unemployment has fallen, 'labour' resistance to change has diminished during the post-war boom. If we do not maintain full employment, and if we lose that new attitude of management to labour which has been induced by scarcity of labour, serious labour resistance, based on fear, will re-emerge.

(*b*) *Ignorance.* Many firms do not know that their methods of production are extremely primitive; or, if they do know, think that they can buy a scientist (on the cheap) who will transmogrify the firm by his very presence.

(*c*) *Indolence.* Some firms know that they are backward, but do nothing about it. In many sectors of industry there is not even enough competition to eliminate the ignorant and indolent.

Indolence (or ignorance) may even exist in our various academies. If so, they will be slow to adjust their conditioning and teaching of children to meet the new technical conditions. Even today many children are trained for the lives they would have lived in the horse and buggy days. Certainly there are some very difficult problems to solve. How many design engineers capable of coping with the advanced mathematics involved in creating automatic control systems are we training? How many scientists, even among those going into management, have received any training in economic and human relations?

I will go no further with my list of impediments. My purpose in listing them is to explain why I do not think the automatic factory is imminent and to help in the preparation of an agenda of obstacles to be overcome. Because there is no good reason to fear 'the age of the automatic factory', it is worth striving to remove these impediments.

I will now summarize some of the main effects of such growth of automatic production and control as we may expect in the near future. This should be seen in the context of the United Kingdom as a trading nation.

(*a*) In the interwar period, the United States, Germany, and Japan gained ground in international trade at the expense of the United Kingdom. The United Kingdom's export industry was for long directed towards meeting the demand of non-industrial countries. This position was undermined by the growth of Japanese competition and a growth of industry in the non-industrial countries. This called for a shift to new types of export based on the newer industries that were expanding in world trade. The United Kingdom's shift to this type of production was too slow.

The foreign trade from which the United Kingdom stands to gain most is trade in goods in which capital per worker and embodied technical knowledge is high. This is the field in which pieces of automation are the condition of production or an indispensable aid in efficient production. The United Kingdom's future in trade, therefore, depends on rapid progress in overcoming the fear, ignorance or indolence that retards the use of automatic controls, and progress in inventing and producing better and cheaper control mechanisms.

The profit from this development is three-fold. There is the export of the product made with the aid of automatic controls, e.g. oil and nuclear products. There is the direct export of the control devices or machines embodying them. There is the saving of imports resulting from the development of the new industries. For example, the growth of the petrochemical industry in this country has made it increasingly possible to provide here the synthetic organic chemicals used in plastics, nylon, detergents, and drugs.

(*b*) The demand for imports tends to increase with greater production and consumption at home. To make possible this higher level of imports, we must increase our exports and that largely depends on a rapid industrial application of science and technology. But full employment also depends on this – slowness in applying science and technology, whether due to an inability or a refusal to apply it, will bring depression in export trades.

Greater production per head itself depends on the industrial application of science and technology and of this automatic control mechanisms are an important part.

(*c*) With the growth of control mechanisms machines have been run at higher speeds and used more fully, wastages have been reduced, the quality of product has been increased. There has been in consequence a fall in the ratio of capital required to produce a unit of output. This 'declining importance of capital', as Colin Clark calls it, does not necessarily mean that we will use less capital in the future than in the present – that depends on how much we want to increase output. It does mean, however, that the capital cost of making output grow is less than it used to be. Offsetting that, the requisite human skill is more than it used to be.

It should be increasingly possible, therefore, for the advanced industrial countries to lend capital to the undeveloped territories. Possibility and interest go hand in hand in this case. Such an export of capital would help both the development of markets for industrial goods and the supply of food and raw materials. This is not, however, a mechanical problem. The lending of capital or the investment of capital in undeveloped territories must be based on agreements to share the benefit, and be accompanied by recognition of an interest in both the social advance of men and the development of markets; otherwise the capital export will create unrest and instability.

At home the implication of the changed capital-output ratio is that we should bring a certain shift in our attention from things to persons. That is to say, we should use up rather more of our material resources and human ingenuity on training and selecting managers, on training and ensuring the best use of scientists, technologists, and technicians, on solving the problem of function, reward, and authority in factories.

These are all difficult problems, but our technical as well as our human advance depend increasingly on solving them.

XIV

Economics in Unwonted Places*

One hundred years ago the President of the Economics and Statistics Section of the British Association was William Farr, MD, FRS. Farr, after a training in medicine, joined the Registrar General's office. He published many papers on general statistics, prepared life tables for insurance, wrote the greater part of the Census Reports of 1851, 1861, and 1871, and resigned when, at the age of seventy-two, he failed to obtain the post of Registrar General.

Farr had a rather naïve belief in the power of statistical tables to solve the difficult problems of political economy, and the power of numerical evidence to determine public policy. In his presidential address he asserted that because 'statistics admits of many practical applications this naturally commends the study to the minds of Englishmen'; that 'the statistical argument in favour of free trade is accumulating; it gains fresh force in every table, and will in the end lead all nations to exchange their products freely'; that statistics 'enables Governments to count the cost of war and to weigh its results against expenses'.

Although much of his approach has a curiously old-fashioned air, his emphasis on the need for 'results-expenses analysis' has not. Cost-benefit analysis, as we now call it, has became very fashionable in academies, and had more notice been taken of Farr's plea for adequate statistical information we would be in a better position to make use of such calculations to guide decisions on public expenditure. Public expenditure is over one-third of national expenditure, but to most of it we cannot apply the market test of whether results (in the form of sales) are greater than the expenses of production. To find out whether the Government should be spending more or less than £450 million on RandD, £1,000 million on education, £250 million on highways, and so on, we have to develop special ways of calculating a results-expenses balance. Failure to take account of this balance leads to the wrong use of resources and to

* Presidential address to Section F at the 1964 meeting of the British Association for the Advancement of Science.

less growth in output per man-hour, and less material satisfaction than we could achieve.

I. COST-BENEFIT ANALYSIS IN THE PUBLIC SECTOR

The modern interest in cost-benefit analysis started, I understand, within the United States Army and then spread to the highway and natural resources engineers. In the United Kingdom the growth of interest has been more recent, and the area of public expenditure for which reasonable cost-benefit calculations have been made is very small indeed.

Owing mainly to the work of the Road Research Board there is now a considerable amount of worthwhile information about the social return to be expected from capital invested in the M1 motorway, the relative merits of investment in new motorways and other road works, and the net social benefits likely to accrue if taxes paid by users of motor vehicles were more closely related to costs of road use. We also have the Beesley-Foster cost-benefit analysis of the new Euston-Victoria line,[1] and the Buchanan report on *Traffic in Towns*, concerned with 'the long-term development of roads and traffic in urban areas, and their influence on the urban environment'. Although Buchanan used an arbitrary 'town planner's' version of cost-benefit analysis, and concentrated on the means and costs of *curing* traffic congestion at the expense of the means and costs of *preventing* it, he produced a very important report; not least because it was commissioned by the Ministry of Transport.

It must be admitted that the cost-benefit analyses of the M1 and the Euston-Victoria line were made after the investment decisions had been made, and that rural motorways still constitute a higher proportion of new road construction than cost-benefit analysis can justify. However, an important start has been made, and perhaps before very long cost-benefit analyses will be undertaken to inform and, we may hope, to improve the decision process.

So far as I know, there are no very good United Kingdom examples of cost-benefit analysis in the fields of defence and health. Nor, despite Adam Smith's ancient demonstration of the similarities between investment in people and investment in machinery, are there good calculations of actual and potential rates of return to investment in education to act as a guide to educational expenditure of various kinds. True, the Robbins and Newsom reports have both produced strong general arguments for believing that the benefits to be gained from greater expenditure on education would exceed the costs. The arguments were, however, too general to provide a useful guide either to short-term priorities in expenditure or to the long-term objectives. For that we need a much more detailed study of the effects of various kinds and lengths of education on both personal development and economic growth.

It would be absurd to suggest that economists and calculators can use cost-benefit analysis to take the difficulty out of decisions to spend on health and education. They cannot. In both cases only part of the expenditure can reasonably be classified as investment. The consumption part – on which for obvious reasons practitioners in both fields tend to place a rather excessive emphasis – throws up problems of valuation which the calculators cannot solve. They can only work out the numerical implications of different value judgements and so make the decision process more informed. They can also calculate the rates of benefit-cost surplus on alternative programmes. Indeed, until this is done, we cannot make sensible choices between alternative uses of scarce resources. We may simply go on believing that there are *right* solutions that we must adopt regardless of cost. This is a form of lunacy which has come to be exposed, though not yet cured, by thought about the problems of expanding rapidly the numbers in higher education.[2]

The application of cost-benefit analysis to expenditure on applied R and D should be rather easier. For unless we equate even applied research to opera and such delights, we can measure the potential benefits in fairly simple commercial terms. However, cost-benefit analysis of public expenditure on applied R and D has developed very slowly. For the most part Government expenditure on R and D has been based on a popular, but quite unproved, belief that if R and D as a percentage of net product is high, that is good for growth. Not only has there been little attempt to measure the benefits,[3] but in measuring the cost of the operation the side effects on the deployment of scarce scientific manpower – which is used both for creating new science and technology and for applying science and technology to industry – have been neglected. The possible significance of this can be demonstrated by a few rough calculations relating to Germany and the United Kingdom. The stock of qualified scientists and engineers is about the same percentage of working population in both countries. But whereas the United Kingdom is spending nearly 3% of net product on R and D, Germany is spending a little over 1%. Allowing for the higher cost per scientist and engineer engaged in

United Kingdom R and D, it appears that the United Kingdom uses twice as many qualified scientists and engineers as Germany in trying to create new science and technology and half as many in trying to *apply* science and technology to industry. There is now a good deal of evidence that the United Kingdom deployment of scientific manpower has actually hindered the rapid application of 'science' to industry. We need scientific manpower to use science in industry, but we need not, and cannot, grow all science at home. To refer to Germany as an example of 'Prosperity Without Science' (as does *The Economist* of 22nd June, 1963) is to misunderstand the whole process. A country may use a great deal of science without making any attempt to add to scientific knowledge by research. A great deal of confusion has resulted from failure to distinguish between the stock of scientific and technological knowledge and the activity of adding to that stock by R and D.

The absence of appropriate cost-benefit analysis shows not only in general Government decisions on public expenditure but also in ministerial decisions on the operation of public enterprises. We can use the case of electricity to illustrate this point.[4] There seems little doubt that the large Government outlay on research has been a factor of importance in decisions on the power plants to be used. The Government made available to the Atomic Energy Authority large sums for the development of nuclear reactors, in the expectation that there would be a handsome pay-off in the form of cost-reducing power stations and export business. In 1955 when coal was expected to remain in short supply it was decided to install 1,500–2,000 MW of nuclear capacity by 1965, and in 1957, when oil supplies were thought to be at risk, this figure was revised to 5,000–6,000 MW. When it became clear that the nuclear reactors would be very far from economic the 5,000 MW programme was extended from 1965 to 1968. Because of these investment decisions, the generating costs of electricity are something like £20 million a year higher than need be.

There appear to be three explanations of this costly policy. First, in the calculations of when nuclear stations would become economic, nuclear engineers made no (or quite insufficient) allowance for progress in the design of conventional stations. This has been, predictably, considerable. Their judgement was as impetuous as that of the English cricket journalists who heard that the Australian team was the weakest on record and took it for granted that England would retain the Ashes. In most interesting things there is more than one variable. The second reason is that the capital cost of nuclear stations is much higher than in conventional stations. Because of this, higher interest rates pushed up nuclear costs more than conventional costs. The third reason, given in the White Paper on nuclear power, is that it has been made 'less economic by the increased emphasis on earning a proper rate of return'. This extraordinary statement needs some explanation. One cost of production is the depreciation of the plant used, which is higher in nuclear than in conventional stations. However, until 1957 the Ministry looked at returns on capital before depreciation.[5] When after 1957 it started to take depreciation into account this constituted a very nasty blow to the estimated economics of nuclear power.

It would be easy to draw up a very long list of cases in the public sector where cost-benefit analysis has been neglected. For instance, the aircraft industry for much of the post-war period had such lavish Government aid that it was responsible for one-third of our total R and D expenditure. Yet it contributed less than 5% to our exports, and nothing spectacular in the way of new technologies to other industries. However, concentration on the public sector would be misleading. For cost-benefit analysis has also been neglected in the private sector, though the neglect has been less publicized.

2. COST-BENEFIT ANALYSIS IN THE PRIVATE SECTOR

There is another good reason to examine cost-benefit analysis in the private sector. This is to make it clear that the basic concept of cost-benefit analysis is not new. It is as old as economics itself. All firms and households are involved in some sort of cost-benefit analysis as part of the normal business of life. The only distinctive thing about the recent growth of cost-benefit analysis is the attempt to measure net social benefits for goods and services that are not sold, or sold under special conditions.

In the classical theory of competition it was supposed that firms would be forced to base their actions on profit calculations. Now these profits are simply the excess of benefits, in the form of revenues from sales, over costs. Profits were given the important functions of providing an incentive to effort and inducing investment in additional capacity where revenues exceeded costs. The important feature of this investment process is that it undermines profits, and so gives firms an incentive to invent new methods or new products. Where one succeeds others copy; the restoration of profits proves short lived;

and the pressure to innovate becomes strong again. The classical economists placed great faith in this built-in pressure to efficiency and innovation. They also assumed that each household knows best how to spend its income and from this followed the conclusion that cost-benefit analysis could be left to firms and households. Thus the whole classical theory of competition implied that firms and households made cost-benefit analyses, and that they based their conduct on them.

But competition does not always exist. Where it does not, making the best use of productive resources requires the guidance of cost-benefit calculations of a kind that are not made by firms as part of the ordinary business of life. The problem of measurement becomes public. Some such measurement is required, for example, whenever the State decides to regulate a monopoly, whether private or public.

In any case, it is now clear that throughout the economy, pressures to efficiency and innovation may not be very strong. The mere presence of many producers, and the absence of agreements to restrict trade, does not ensure such action.[6] Impressive evidence of a large degree of slack in the United Kingdom economy is to be found in the files of industrial consultants. When Professor J. Johnston examined a sample from these files, he found that where quantitative assessments were both feasible and recorded consultants were able to suggest lines of actions which brought average productivity increases of over 50%.[7]

Now it is true that the use of industrial consultants (and of internal operational research teams) costs money, a fact which cost-benefit analysis must take into account. But there is plenty of evidence that in thousands of firms a cost-benefit analysis would show the wisdom of incurring the cost.

Further striking evidence comes from a recent publication by the British Productivity Council, *Sixteen Studies in Value Analysis*. 'Value analysis', a technique said to have originated in the General Electric Company of the United States, is a form of cost-benefit analysis. Many firms use 'work study' in an effort to cut production costs of a given product. Value analysis simply goes further by not taking the product as given. It analyses the product's function, and then seeks the minimal costs of providing for that function. The return on the cost of the value analysis is often very high. In one United States defence programme the return was sixty times the cost. The United Kingdom studies suggest a typical return of twelve to fifteen times the cost.

What of the more general search for new methods which competition is supposed to ensure? Do typical firms give enough attention to it? C. F. Carter and I looked into this for the Science and Industry Committee (formed at the Belfast meeting of the British Association), and we reported in *Industry and Technical Progress* that they do not.

This is a complex matter. In some industries the search cannot go far without a large outlay on R and D; in other industries it is the inventions of others (of, for example, the makers of machines, machine tools, scientific instruments, chemicals) which matter. But even in the science-based industries, R and D expenditure alone is not enough. Both the choice of worthwhile projects and the final application of science to industry depend on having qualified scientists and technologists in production departments. Furthermore, even in industries with high rates of expenditure on R and D, many of the opportunities for innovation come from outside the firm – from another industry or country. In all industries, then, it is important to watch for outside changes and to identify opportunities, and this also requires skilled scientists and engineers. Within firms, as well as nationally, too little thought has been given to the best use of scientific manpower, and there has been insufficient attention to costs and benefits in alternative uses.

Competition is also supposed to force firms to invest in all projects where, after allowance for risk, the prospective rate of return over cost is greater than the relevant rate of interest. Yet the upshot of many inquiries into investment decisions is that relatively few firms, even in the competitive sector, so act. [8]

Some firms do not even calculate the prospective rate of return over cost, preferring to take action only if 'the case is so obvious that calculation is rather pointless'. This must mean that they miss many worthwhile investment projects. The majority appear to use a pre-tax average rate of return above cost, in association with a minimum rate of return which they find acceptable. It is remarkable how often this pass or cut-off rate proves to be 15%. Yet a 15% cut-off rate of return is arbitrary, and even in a given period it is irrational to use a 15% cut-off rate for both replacement of plant with hardly any interruption of earnings, and investment in a new product which takes several years to work up to a profitable rate of output.

The calculation of pre-tax benefit is also misleading. The impact of initial allowances, investment allowances and development-area grants can vary greatly between projects with the ratio of fixed to total capital and the location of the investment. A cash-flow analysis concerned with the present value of prospective receipts and payments (including tax), and not a pre-tax average yield calculation, is needed. The failure to use a cash-flow analysis has led both to the choice of many wrong projects and to an under-estimation of the profitability of investment, particularly in re-equipment. A sudden shift to cash-flow analysis would probably face the Chancellor with an embarrassingly abrupt investment boom.

3. SOCIAL AND PRIVATE COSTS

I come now to a different sort of cost-benefit problem, elaborated by Marshal and Pigou. Differences between social and private costs (and benefits) call for some sort of public control over the commercial activities of firms, whether public or private. If smoke from factory chimneys inflicts an unchanged loss on the community as injury to health, buildings and plants, and expenses for cleaning, the social costs will be greater than the costs to the firms concerned. So too with alcoholic liquor if the costs of alcoholism, road accidents and the additional police and magistrates due to drunkenness are not charged to the industry. So too with tobacco if its side costs in the form of lung cancer and heart disease are not charged. If a transport firm used the Queen's Highway quite free its own costs would be less than the social cost to the extent of the physical deterioration of the highway and the additional road congestion.

By contrast, a firm that spends money on training or research may get less benefit from them in the form of lower costs or greater sales than does the community. For the trained labour may go to another firm, and research may lead to new processes or products which other firms adopt, without paying to the firm that incurred the cost the difference between the return to the firm and the return to the community.

Where social and private costs differ, and these differences are not the same in each industry, the competitive system can only allocate productive resources properly if taxes and bounties offset these differences. Otherwise production will be too large where private cost is less than social cost, and vice versa.

Little attention has been given to the *measurement* of differences between social and private costs and benefits for, e.g. alcohol and tobacco. Of course, excise duties on tobacco and alcohol are high, and until fairly recently it probably seemed obvious that they more than covered the difference between social and private cost. However, with the rise in the incidence of lung cancer and heart diseases and the growing evidence of widespread alcoholism, this should no longer be taken for granted. A systematic statistical study is needed. In saying this I do not imply that we should simply measure the loss of earnings and medical costs due to drug addiction and throw that cost on the industries. Where prohibition is not appropriate (as with smoke nuisance) a great deal of medical research and health education is called for, and this should be included in the social cost.

For road transport, efforts have been made to calculate whether parking and licence fees, and petrol duties, do compensate for the differences between private and social costs. These differences vary between country, trunk, and city roads. Transport economists have insisted that because taxes on road transport do not conform to these differences, potential social gains are there to be gathered in by an appropriate system of pricing. Recently the Ministry of Transport appointed an expert committee to examine the economic and technical possibilities of pricing road use according to costs. The committee concluded that practical pricing methods could probably be devised and that the measurable net gain to the community would be in the order of £100–£150 million a year. There is much more work to be done in the field, but *Road Pricing* is a most encouraging start.

Where social benefits are greater than private benefits, a case can be made for bounties. Industrial expenditures on research and training are assumed to generate a social-benefit surplus and are given favourable tax treatment, though little effort has been made to measure the assumed surplus. I have come to doubt whether there is a general social-benefit surplus from industrial research. Given our very large research expenditure and low growth, and the signs that we have placed excessive emphasis on the use of scientific manpower in research, we should consider whether blanket tax allowances for research have contributed to that maldistribution. I suspect that they have, though the effect is likely to be very much smaller than that of large Government research grants to particular industries made without the aid of cost-benefit calculation.

4. WHY THE NEGLECT?

The neo-classical theory that, subject only to differences between private and social costs, firms in following their own interests would promote the public good, was not based on the idea of a spontaneous harmony of interests. The theory was only applied to competitive conditions. It was based on the idea that competition would force firms to act as if there were an identity of interests. Competition is simply a form of social control. In the absence of competiton we need other forms of social control.

Competition is now a less pervasive form of social control than in the nineteenth century. The reason is that technical conditions of production have changed. The folk wisdom contained in the saying 'necessity is the mother of invention' has been weakened by the change in the nature of invention. Nowadays typical inventions grow out of expensive applied R and D activities (not necessarily at home), which in turn grow out of expensive processes of higher education and pure research. For the inventive process we cannot now rely on competition. If the State creates the basic conditions by providing for education, basic research and even applied R and D where there is reason to expect a 'pay-off' but the necessary scale cannot be managed by the public or private firms in the industry, then competitive pressures can play an important part in the speedy and efficient application of science to industry.

Once the basic conditions of industrial innovation are provided for, it is quite possible to have strong competition with only a few producers. But without a strong sense of opportunities to innovate, and at least a suspicion that competitors know how and intend to use them, competitive pressure, even in multi-firm industries, is not likely to be strong. In this case there is bite in the quip that competition is not severe because businessmen only have to compete with other businessmen.

In some industries it is not simply the conditions of invention that have changed, but also the conditions for exploiting inventions. The scale of expenditure involved in developing, for example, a supersonic airliner is such that the United Kingdom and France found it necessary to venture jointly. In atomic power it is beginning to seem that we should have ventured jointly. Going it alone forced what may prove to be a very expensive gamble on the most likely form of nuclear development.

Although competition cannot be such a pervasive and creative form of social control as it used to be, we have not created an effective substitute for it. This is because far too few people have realized that competition is an effective form of social control only if competitive pressure is associated with an opportunity to innovate. From the need for greater Government action to create the conditions of effective competition in a wide range of industries, and the need for new forms of social control in sectors of industry (including much of the public sector) where the competitive mechanism cannot operate, follows the need for a radical overhaul of the Government machinery. The Civil Service, as at present organized and manned, cannot cope with many of the problems of modern industry.[9] I have emphasized the need for more cost-benefit analysis to guide decisions. Such cost-benefit analysis may often be very complicated indeed, and require the co-operation of scientists, technologists, economists, and statisticians to provide the basic detailed information and expert judgements on which the forecasts should be based.

The need for a more adequate provision 'for the organized acquisition of facts and information, and for the systematic application of thought, as preliminary to the settlement of policy and its subsequent administration' was emphasized in the Haldane Report on the Machinery of Government (Command Paper 9230, 1918). On the grounds of 'the proved impracticability of devoting the necessary time to thinking out organization and the preparation for action in the mere interstices of the time required for the transaction of business' (para. 13), the Haldane Committee recommended (para. 14) that: (i) in all departments better provision should be made for inquiry, research, and reflection before policy is defined and put into operation, and (ii) that for some purposes the necessary research and inquiry should be carried out and supervised by a Department of Government specially charged with these duties, but working in the closest contact with the administrative departments concerned with its activities.

The establishment under the Lord President of the Council of the D S I R to develop and organize the knowledge required for the application of science to industry was in accordance with part (ii) of this Haldane doctrine. But apart from small statistical sections within some departments and the post-war creation of the C S O, part (i) of the doctrine was practically ignored. Not surprisingly, therefore, departments are badly placed to perform the tasks which fall to them. For example, the Ministry of Transport as at present constituted and manned is not competent to make cost-benefit calculations and is badly placed to make wise long-term decisions about inland transport policy. It has no research section itself and has to rely for advice on the Road Research Laboratory of D S I R, the research organs of the airlines (under the Ministry of Aviation), and British Railways. The

Ministry of Power is no better placed – perhaps worse placed in that the activities of the AEA (which include the final development of nuclear reactors) are matters for the Ministry of Science.[10]

There is a further problem which is well illustrated by the private proposals to dam Morecambe Bay and Solway Firth. Here are two projects having little hope of acceptance without a wide-ranging public cost-benefit analysis. These dams would create vast supplies of fresh water and give a good line for a northern motorway avoiding Shap. They would greatly improve the prospects of depressed areas in North-West Lancashire and West Cumberland, and create an excellent opportunity for new town developments. Yet, such projects very seldom originate from the public sector, and when they come up are simply referred to interdepartmental committees which lack the ability and the will to evaluate them. This doubtless helps to explain why the United Kingdom has such a poor record in resource development. Despite our less doctrinaire attitude to Government intervention, we have not produced anything remotely like the Tennessee Valley Authority.

The related failure to develop public cost-benefit analysis of possible lines of action and to adapt our social controls to new technologies, is an important part of the explanation of our failures in economic growth. So, too, is straightforward lack of understanding of a kind that can be cured by investment in the appropriate forms of education, so long, of course, as we manage to sell the potential output to the right people. When businessmen and civil servants choose investment criteria which are not in the interests of growth in output per head it is not always because they have offsetting interests. It is often because they don't know better.

It is now accepted that we need a great increase in business education. But the magnitude of the problem is such that it cannot be left to a few business schools who will take in students at the post-graduate stage and after ten years in industry. Training in appropriate forms of cost-benefit analysis in, for example, the engineering schools will be every bit as important. And, if we are to move quickly, educating the existing top managers and administrators will be even more important. There is room at the top for a great deal of education in the uses that can be made of modern techniques for making plans, choosing rationally from among them, and exercising control; room also for education in the conditions required for the proper use of these techniques.

When the British Association programme was printed I was

asked several times whether the 'unwonted' in the title of my address was a misprint for 'unwanted'. It was not, though I doubt whether it would have mattered. Strong resistances to cost-benefit analysis come from those who fear that such analysis might lead to a smaller expenditure on what they are interested in, from those who are used to making decisions in situations where 'quick decisions are more important than right decisions' (though the need for a quick decision is frequently the result of failure to think ahead), and from those who desire to operate within a given administrative framework, even when that administrative framework is too restricted for the problem in hand. This is not surprising. But given that our resources cannot be stretched to do all the things we would like, there is a continuing need to discover and explain the costs and benefits of different lines of action, and to see that our social control systems help resources to flow into the appropriate channels.

5. POSTSCRIPT

There have been several changes in structure and process of Government as affecting Government interest in 'science and industry' since I wrote this paper.

In the main, the sensible principle of attaching Government Research Stations to the Ministry with a direct interest in the use of results has been followed.[11] The Road Research Laboratory and the Building Research Station were transferred from the DSIR to the departments with the relevant operational responsibility – namely, the Ministry of Transport and the Ministry of Public Buildings and Works. The other Research Stations of the DSIR, together with responsibility for the Research Associations, were taken over by the new Ministry of Technology (with which the Ministry of Aviation, and its Research Stations, was recently merged), which acquired a sponsoring responsibility for the most relevant industries.

There are, however, two significant exceptions from the principle of attaching a Government Research Station to the Ministry with the operational responsibility for the industry. The Department of Education and Science, and not the Ministries of Health and Agriculture, was given responsibility for both the Medical and Agricultural Research Councils, perhaps reasonably because of the high proportion of pure research conducted by the Councils, the interest of the Department in 'teaching hospitals', the high level of R and D conducted by pharmaceutical firms, and the role of the National

Agricultural Advisory Service in an industry where segregated research presents fewest problems.

Responsibility for the Atomic Energy Authority was transferred from the Lord President to the Ministry of Technology, although the Authority's civil output is mainly relevant to the activities of the Ministry of Power, and its non-civil output to the Ministry of Defence. Here part of the explanation is that the Minister of Technology was given power to direct the Authority to undertake applied R and D work outside the field of atomic energy, presumably in the hope both that new work could be found to offset the declining need for atomic energy research, and that the highly skilled staff of the Authority could successfully create other new technologies. So far neither the Ministry of Technology nor the Authority appear to have discovered any projects which would justify a substantial expenditure. It is not difficult to find research problems which come within the spheres of the Science or National Environment Research Councils. It is much more difficult to find applied R and D problems which are likely to have an appropriate impact on economic growth and would be best done by the Authority. The key difficulty is that the segregation of R and D from production and marketing only works well when the technological goal is clear – such as, for example, to produce an atomic reactor capable of making cheaper power than a conventional reactor. And even here, as we have seen, once the basic inventions are made the subsequent improvements in production technology may be hindered by a continued segregation of R and D from production. The solution here, at any rate for reactor systems subsequent to the Advanced Gas-cooled Reactor, may be to push the reactor, production and engineering groups of the Atomic Energy Authority – employing over half the present staff – much closer to the production and marketing of nuclear reactors.

What of changes in the process of Government? It is no longer true to say that the Ministry of Transport is constituted and manned in such a way that it is not competent to make cost benefit calculations. There is now a Director-General of Economic Planning, with appropriate staff, responsible for such calculations. In the Ministry of Power work has begun on the input-output models of the fuel sector of the economy required for cost benefit analyses on which fuel policies should be based. The position on resource development has also improved. The Ministry of Land and Natural Resources and the Water Resources Board (set up in fact in 1963) have commissioned cost-benefit studies of barrages.

The Ministry of Defence – to which, along with the Ministry of Aviation, my comments about the need to use modern techniques for making plans, choosing rationally from among them, and exercising control, were particularly relevant – has introduced ten-year forward budgeting and functional costing on the lines of the US Defence Secretariat, and a Defence Operational Analysis Establishment. Whether, however, the Ministry, with its divisions between the administrative and scientific classes, has created the conditions for the successful use of planning and control techniques is to be doubted. In the new Ministry of Technology much has been done to desegregate the functions of the administrative and scientific classes, and a techno-economic programmes appraisal unit has been set up (jointly with the Atomic Energy Authority) and further appraisal work is envisaged in the general Economics and Statistics Division.

Merging the Ministry of Aviation with the Ministry of Technology, with its wider industrial functions and interests, should bring a check to the very costly habit of treating aircraft research, development and design capacity as an output of the economic system, and, in view of the suitable occasion provided by big changes in the structure of the aircraft industry, a re-appraisal of the scope and role of the Government Aircraft Research Establishments. There will of course be a continuing temptation in a ministry responsible directly for a large expenditure on research establishments to treat Government R and D as a good thing in itself, and to place in them R and D contracts which would be better placed in industrial firms. Conscious of this danger and of its other role in encouraging the spread of technology throughout industry, the Ministry has created a strong engineering group alongside the research group. Within this set-up the main problem will be to create an appropriate decision mechanism which will ensure that the technological objectives of the Ministry will be reflected in the separate decisions taken in this very large ministry. Here the traditional Civil Service management structure – described by Professor P.M.S. Blackett recently as the $1:3:n$ structure – may prove to be a serious weakness.

There have then been some welcome changes since I wrote. Awareness of the problem has certainly increased, but there is a vast amount still to be done in adjusting Civil Service procedures, recruitment and appointments. In short, some very welcome swallows but far too few as yet to bring a summer.

REFERENCES

1. See, for example, *Road Research Technical Papers* 46 and 48 (1960) and BE 246 (1963); *Road Pricing* (Ministry of Transport (1964); C. FOSTER and M. BEESLEY, 'Estimating the Social Benefit from Constructing an Underground Railway in London', *Journal of the Royal Statistical Society* (1963).

2. I have examined some of the implications of treating universities as multi-product firms in 'Capacity and Output of Universities', *The Manchester School* (May 1963). For some of the financial implications of this form of analysis see C. F. CARTER and B. R. WILLIAMS, 'Proposals for Reform in University Finance', *The Manchester School* (September 1963).

3. For an attempt, see R. EWELL *Chemical and Engineering News* (1955), pp. 2,980–6. For critical analysis see F. MACHLUP, *The Production and Distribution of Knowledge in the United States* (Princeton University Press, 1963); and B. R. WILLIAMS, *Investment and Technology in Growth* (Manchester Statistical Society, 1964).

4. The reports of the Select Committee on Nationalized Industries make it clear that investment decisions have often been irrational. For an analytical summary of practices and a comment on the rather mixed-up White Paper on 'The Financial and Economic Obligations of the Nationalized Industries' (Command Paper 1337) see A. J. MERRETT and A. SYKES, 'The Financial Control of State Industry', *The Banker* (March and April 1962).

5. See Report and Proceedings of the Select Committee on Nationalized Industries: Electricity Supply Industry. In answer to questions 155–7, it emerged that the Ministry looked for a gross and not net return on average net assets 'to give credit to an industry like the electricity supply industry which had a more prudent depreciation policy'.

6. I examined the reasons in a paper read at the British Association meeting in York, and later published in the *Yorkshire Bulletin of Economic and Social Studies* (December 1959) (Chapter VI).

7. 'The Productivity of Management Consultants', *Journal of the Royal Statistical Society* (1963).

8. For some recent evidence see *Report of the Committee on Turnover Taxation* (Command Paper 2300, HMSO, 1964). See also P. W. S. ANDREWS and E. BRUNNER, *Capital Development in Steel* (Blackwell, 1951); C. F. CARTER and B. R.

WILLIAMS, *Industry and Technical Progress* (Oxford University Press, 1957); and Chapter X.

9. There is now a considerable literature on the shortcomings of the Civil Service. See, for example, B. CHAPMAN, *British Government Observed* (Allen & Unwin, 1963). See also P. D. HENDERSON, 'The Use of Economists in British Administration', Oxford Economic Papers (1961); and A. J. MERRETT and A. SYKES, op. cit.

10. See para. 402 of the Report of the Select Committee on Nationalized Industries: Electricity Supply Industry, where it is reported that when the AEA decided to build a particular prototype of a heavy water reactor the CEGB was not told in advance. When it expressed misgivings and asked how the Authority evaluated schemes in competition with others the Authority declined to show the papers. When the Ministry of Power took up the matter with the Authority it was simply told that the Authority and not the CEGB was charged with the responsibility to develop nuclear reactors.

11. See C. F. CARTER and B. R. WILLIAMS, 'Government Scientific Policies and the Growth of the British Economy', *The Manchester School* (September 1964).